Ontological Mysticism

An Experience of God

Ontological Mysticism

An Experience of God

by

Ben Gilberti

One Spirit Press
Portland, Oregon

One Spirit Press
www.onespiritpress.com
Portland, Oregon

Dedication

This book is dedicated to my beloved mother, who truly was one of the most magnificent women who has ever lived.

Acknowledgment

I wish to thank my whole famly, my mother and father– Rose and Ben, and my sisters and brother Joe,
Marie and Maureen for all their amazing support, and
especially for helping me through all my trials and
tribulations.

Contents

Truth & Mesmerism **3** • *Practicing the Presence of God* **7**

Going Beyond the Brink **15** • *The Monumental Lie* **19**

Most Delicate Power of All **25** • *Nothingize the Parent* **31**

From External Forms to Internal Formlessness **39** •

Face the Bully Eye to Eye **43** • *The Divine Flower* **47**

Death and Ecstasy **51** • *All There Is is You* **55**

In God's Heaven **59** •

The Spiritual Application of E=mc² **65**

The Hallucinations of Duality **75** • *Self-Confrontation* **81**

Time Out **87** • *Self Deception* **93**

The Most Dangerous Idea in the World **103**

"Be Still, and Know that I am God" **111**

Nothingizing the Dual Mode of Perception **121**

The Space Between Thoughts **127**

God's Will and Lucifer's **133**

God's Will and Yours **139**

The Brick **147**

Cosmic Intention: Infinity Resonating as Finite Definition **151**

Terror, Intimacy and the Sacred **155**

Kiss and Make Up **161**

How to Begin to Experience Yourself as God **167**

Conclusion: Open Your Awareness to Infinity **173**

Introduction

Everyone who knows anything about Mysticism, knows that the full realization of God cannot be attained through thoughts or words. The Archetype of the Story of Exodus provides a paradigm of spiritual development that includes "spiritualized intellect" symbolized by Moses. In the archetype, Moses is essential to the spiritual development process, leading the chosen people out of slavery in Egypt to the brink of the Promised Land. Egypt represents the paradigm of duality. The Promised Land represents the realization of Oneness or God. But Moses does not enter himself, because even the most spiritualized intellect could never comprehend God. He does lead to the brink, however, which is where one needs to be to go beyond intellect and actually experience God.

The following is an exercise in spiritualized intellect leading to the brink of the experience of God.

The Presence of God

"The principle can be summarized quite clearly and simply. Anything other than that which is, is not.

"

Ontological Mysticism   Ben Gilberti

Truth & Mesmerism

The Truth is that God is all there is. There simply is nothing else. The appearance of anything else (like pain, distress, disease, misfortune, poverty, crime, war, hatred, fear, etc.) is nothing but the mesmerism that grows out of the mistaken belief that something else besides God could exist. The miracles of Jesus Christ, or the miraculous healings of modern day mystics, occur by deliberately knowing the Truth right in the midst of the mesmerisms caused by the beliefs in something other than Truth.

This is not easy to do because we are so surrounded by the mesmerism. It is necessary that we learn to become very still so that the self-evident certainty that God is all there is can emerge.

The principle can be summarized quite clearly and simply. Anything other than that which is, is not. And hence that which is, is all there is, because all else is not. And since that which is is all there is, it is therefore entire, total, complete, whole, one, harmonious, perfect, absolute, infinite and eternal (or, in other words, God). And since God is all there is, there cannot be anything at all that is less than, or other than, or opposed to God. Since awareness necessarily must exist in order for you

3

to know this, then awareness, the pure "I," must be God.

But even though the logic of it is simple, clear and certain, the sheer magnitude of its implications require that we become aware of a highly intimate inner knowing that we can discover only in silent contemplation. Indeed if God is all there is, all that "I" can be is God. We must become still enough to know this to be true in the most intimate way imaginable, to sink in meditation past all the pandemonious mesmerisms about ourselves until we arrive at that absolute center of consciousness where "I" and God (the sole reality that is all there is) are one and the same.

Do it now. Close your eyes. Become still and quietly know that God is all there is and all there ever can be, and then become completely silent so that you can know this at a depth deeper than words or thoughts.

Now, if you will simply do that every hour of the day, the mesmerism will continually subside, and you will become more and more an oasis of True Godliness to those still believing in the mesmerisms.

Once you dehypnotize yourself out of the trance of experiencing yourself as a being less than the fullness of God, you will know yourself as you actually are -- the living Truth being all that it is. And even though the universal mesmerism that creates the vast dream of humanity may linger, your effect within that dream will be to catalyze, through the inspiration of what your life in the dream will become, the desire and ability to awaken on the part of those aspects of yourself who, in the dream, still appear to be "others." You will be an effective agent in the symphonic rising crescendo of the Great Awakening wherein all of humanity, and all consciousness everywhere, will let go of all illusions and realize and experience the entire universe as the one infinite consciousness you now only dimly refer to as God.

Layer by layer you let go of every sense of selfhood that falls short of God's nature. At the same time becoming more clearly aware that God's nature is all you possibly can be. The spiritualized intellect thus leads you, like Moses, to the brink of the promised land, and, like Moses, must stay behind as you take the final step of realizing that the absolute center of your consciousness, the I of you before it forms itself into "I am this particular human being," the pure I as awareness itself rather than any form, concept or perception that awareness may at any time be aware of, that absolutely pure center of your consciousness, is nothing less than God, appearing to be much less than that only to the extent you insist that "I am limited, human, isolated, vulnerable, etc."

Evermore do you more clearly realize that this one God that can be the only reality anywhere, this one God that is entire, total complete, perfect, absolute and infinite, is the "I" of you before your erroneous beliefs distract you from the Truth. As you let go of the erroneous beliefs, less and less do they distract you, and as the distractions subside, in the stillness they leave behind, you discover the "I" you always have been and always will be, the "I" that is, like Melchizedec, "without mother, without father, without beginning or end of days," the I of you that says to the cacophony of your distractions, "Be Still, and Know that I am God," the I of you that says "I and the Father are one."

"The principle, clearly, is that there cannot be anything other than God. "

Practicing the Presence of God

You practice the presence of God by intending to see God everywhere you look, and by intending to be God in action in everything that you do, and by intending to be absolutely open to omniscience, wisdom, grace, love and inspiration beyond anything that your finite perspective could even imagine.

What do you do about the lingering habitual actions that do not originate from God? They have no power, no reality. They are nothing and you treat them as nothing. You give them no attention whatever. Instead all of your attention is poised to receive divine inspiration. So you live life and enjoy it, but every moment you are aware of one thing and one thing only -- only God is present here. That is practicing the Presence of God, and it's your job here.

How do you live in-between meditations? Well, between meditations consist of nothing but a continuous present moment. In this present moment, that is always present no matter whether you are talking to someone, writing, eating, cooking or meditating, in this continuously present present moment, you are present as one thing and one thing alone, you are present as awareness. You are not present as worries, fears, irritations or doubts. No, the only reason you can be aware of those kinds of things is that you are present as something altogether different -- awareness, that which says, "I".

What is it really that constitutes this miracle of awareness? How is it that you are aware? Did you manufacture this ability of yours to be aware? No. But somehow it's always been there. All the while this awareness of yours didn't seem to be anything greatly wondrous because up to now you have mostly been aware of all manner of suffering. But now, you are aware of something quite different than all this. Now you are aware of a principle -- something that is self-evidently true at all times and in all places -- an absolute truth -- That God is all there is, Truth is all there is. There cant be anything other than Truth. In in order for it to be something other than Truth, it would of necessity have to be Not Truth. In being not Truth, it necessarily has to be not so. Hence Truth has to be all there is besides which there cannot possibly be anything else. This then makes Truth in being all there is, entire, total, complete, whole, one, harmonious, perfect, absolute, infinite and eternal, which is probably the best definition of God that words can provide -- all of this you are now aware of.

You can't see it, touch it, taste it, handle it, or measure it. You are clearly aware of its claim to be the only thing that is real and the only thing that can be real. And it is *your* awareness that is aware of this. The principle clearly is that there cannot *be* anything other than God. Your awareness of necessity *must be* in order for it to be aware of this principle. And so there you are awareness, clearly aware of a principle that says it is absolutely impossible that you exist as anything other than God. It's your awareness that's aware of this, not anything else about yourself, not your fears, doubts, limitations, desires or confusions, but simply your awareness. And what is it now that the principle says it possible for awareness to be aware of? The only thing that can exist -- God. So there you are aware of all that.

At the same time, when you come out of your meditation, you find your awareness keenly aware of an identity you have assumed as a human being who is among a community of similar identities all working hard at maintaining the comfortable survival of that identity. So what do you do?

Well, what would God do if He were to find Himself in your predicament? What would God do if it were God Himself, absolute, infinite, perfect consciousness, who just now realized that He had been asleep in a dream for 40 years and was now sitting in this chair after having just realized who He was in a meditation and was now faced with the necessity of *doing* something *in the dream*. Yes, of course, God wouldn't even be in the dream, *but you are* and now you have to get up from your meditation in your dream body and *do something*. So what would *God do* if He were in your shoes?

This is a world of action. What action would God take? Would God shout out to others that God is all there is? Is that what God would do if He got up in your body after a meditation? Would He confuse everyone by disappearing mysteriously or flaring out in a ball of light? Would he call up his boss at work and say, "Listen, I realize I'm God now so I won't be needing to work for the likes of you anymore."

One thing that He would do is quietly heal everyone

who asked for healing. And He would really listen to people. Really listen to them. You'll be surprised how often people are asking you for healing. By healing we mean investing your time and attention to realizing the nothingness of every claim of distress in the light of the oneness and allness of God. This is something you do. More than that it is something you give. You can give people many things which they will enjoy receiving, like a wonderful meal, or a sympathetic ear, or warmth and affection, or loyal friendship, but the greatest gift you can give anyone, and one they will enjoy inestimably more than any other, is the gift of always seeing them as they truly are -- God in manifestation. Now it doesn't really matter what else you are doing as long as you are doing that.

What else would God do? If God were with someone else, would God sit there staring into space inwardly knowing that this person sitting next to him is God too? God certainly would know that the only thing worth doing is to help this person awaken to the fact that he is God too. But would God grab the guy by the scruff of the neck and say, "Listen, you really need to snap out of this, you're not a limited human, you're God!"

The real question is what God would do if he fell asleep to the fact he was God. And was just beginning to wake up, still finding himself in a half-asleep stupor of habitual desires to do all kinds of things. What would God do if he found himself in that precise situation?

When you ask yourself that question, you will get an answer, always, because you are asking the right question of the right source. The only source of the answer can be God. It is the right question because it is the exact question that your entire life is an answer to. Everything you ever do is your answer to the question at that time. It just depends on how asleep you are at the time. If you're sound asleep you don't hear the question at all. As you begin to awaken, the question at first almost feels like an unwelcome intrusion into otherwise comfortable areas of your life. And indeed at first you awaken a little only to fall back asleep again. But as you awaken more and more, this question becomes evermore present throughout your day. What would God do if He found himself in this precise situation I am in right here and now? Would God condemn for whatever was done in the past? Would God smother the person next to him with a lot of "human love?" Would God be silent and ominously aloof? Would God frighten people with wizardry?

Keep in mind that we are talking about what God would do if he were *exactly* in your predicament. If he, in-other-words, found himself just as you do with an entire brain full of erroneous beliefs and a severe habit of supporting his conviction in those beliefs on the basis of appearances that grow out of the beliefs. If he found himself just as you do in a world of billions of himself that were, except for a rare few, completely asleep to the truth about who and what they are. If he found himself in a world just as you do where waking up from the dream is extremely rare, and where those who have done so are revered as unattainably lofty Ascended Masters.

The more you contemplate the question, the more you realize that this is precisely what you are right now. You are God having fallen asleep and just now beginning to wake up, and so you are the exactly perfect being to ask this question of. So when you ask yourself this question, you are asking the right source. You are God and you have been so sound asleep to that fact that you are God that even as you are now beginning to wake up the whole idea seems difficult to grasp, and almost everyone you know is continually trying to get you to go back to sleep. At first you do turn back into the slumber. But each time you do, the good/evil paradigm of the dream eventually hits you with its evil side, and when you roll up your sleeves to "nothingize" the distress, you remind yourself again about who and what you are, and you begin to wake up again.

Eventually you become very interested in paying close attention to what goes on in your awareness as your days unfold moment by moment. And eventually you realize that at any moment, you are either waking up by knowing that God is the only presence in that moment, or you are going back to sleep by "forgetting" that God is present. Eventually, you are always aware of the fact that anything you think, say, do, or feel is your answer to the question, "What would God do if He were in your shoes?"

On thing is certain -- God would fill His life with giving the greatest gift that can be given -- the recognition of everyone's absolute Godliness, and everything else he did, like making coffee in the morning, would be in honor of that. *The Course in Miracles* puts it well, "Teach only love for that is what you are." The way you make coffee in the morning is teaching something, to yourself and to others. The way you do anything is teaching yourself and others something. What is it teaching? What you do about having done something that taught something other than love will again be teaching something. What you do about having done something that taught something other than love *can* teach you, and others, love. You eventually come to the place where you always forgive everyone, including yourself, for absolutely everything. You finally realize that unloving behavior is nothing, and when you do you find that you have no desire for nothing. You don't condemn yourself for desiring anything other than God, you realize instead that all you ever really did desire was God.

The most important part of all this is to realize that God is. Feel what it feels like for God to be all there is in absolute fullness everywhere now. Feel what it feels like for you to be right now absolutely all that God is. That which isn't, isn't either good or bad, it simply isn't. That which is, isn't divided up into good and bad but is in it's entirety God. Feel what it feels like that right now, right this very instant, God is absolutely and completely all there is everywhere. Why pay any attention at all to appearances to the contrary when you know full well that there cannot be anything contrary. Give up feeling what it feels like for the appearances to be real. Now you know they're not. So instead of giving any attention whatsoever to any appearances of reality being even the slightest bit less than God, simply feel what it feels like for God to be all there is right now.

You surrender yourself to that which you do not yet comprehend.

Ontological Mysticism   Ben Gilberti

Going Beyond the Brink

Now, if you have been following along with all this, it is by now clear to you that all that is written here cannot of itself create the experience of God. All of the above is only Moses leading you to the brink of the Promised Land -- God. Yes, God is all there is, that is the principle, but what that really means it totally beyond comprehension. Any idea you can possible have of it must necessarily fall far short of what God actually IS. You cannot dream God up in your mind. Neither do you need to because God already IS.

Infinite beingness is incomprehensible to all save itself. It is only as you surrender your entire self to God that you come to know God. This means that if you have not yet surrendered entirely to God, you do not yet know God. You do not know what God is, but only that whatever God is he is all there is. And if God is all there is then there isn't anything else about you that is real. So you surrender yourself to that which you do not yet comprehend. You no longer demand to comprehend before you surrender because you now know that the Allness of God is so absolute, so limitless, so infinite, it would be impossible for you, as long as you continue to identify with anything other than God, to comprehend it. And yet you do know that God most certainly is, and most certainly is *all* there is, and therefore is infinitely perfect.

What this all means is that reality is infinitely better than even your grandest and wildest hopes and dreams. When the grace of God flows through your life it becomes infinitely more enjoyable, delightful, wondrous and ecstatic than anything you could even imagine. This is what you must accept when you realize that God is all there is. It seems altogether far, far too good to be true! And in fact it is *true*. So much, in fact, is it infinitely better than anything you desire in the dream world, that you could delay your awakening for eons and create for yourself the most dreadful illusions of separation from God and all of it won't matter to you one jot when you finally realize, accept and surrender to the fact that God is all there is.

Any separation from God, even in the slightest degree, is totally and completely an illusion. But you cannot really say "I am God" unless you have completely surrendered to God and melted *completely* into *him*. Why? God is *completely one* not almost completely one, but *completely one*. So you cannot in fact be even the slightest bit separate from God.

And so Moses keeps nudging us, "There it is folks, the Promised Land, I've taken you as far as I can go, and now you are going to have to go where your human comprehension cannot accompany you, you will have to *trust* that God is your supply, your energy, your life, your intelligence, your ability, your wisdom, your love, your joy, your peace, your guidance, your insight and your heart."

Anything even the slightest bit other than God is absolutely impossible and never happened at all.

The Monumental Lie

If an appearance is an illusion, then it is a lie. It is claiming to exist and it doesn't. It is claiming something that is not true. So it is a lie.

It's impossible to lie about nothing. A lie, in order for it to be a lie, must be lying about truth. So you greet each appearance with the question, "What is the truth that this appearance is lying about?" The answer of course is always the only Truth there is -- God being all there is. God is *infinite* beingness manifesting *infinitely* right now. So the *only* thing you ever *could* see is God's infinite manifestation. What is going on when you see what you call an "appearance?" You wouldn't be calling it an appearance unless it was something that claimed to be less than or contrary to God. But who or what is making such a claim? Is it the *appearance* that is actually *doing* this? Is the appearance something out there existing external to you that somehow has a life and existence of its own apart from you? Of course not. You, yourself, are every moment creating the appearance by making the claim yourself that something less than or contrary to God is *possible*.

Anything even the slightest bit other than God is absolutely *impossible* and *never happened at all*. There isn't now, nor has there ever been, anything happening anywhere that wasn't God being God's infinite self. You aren't in the business of using truth or God or mysticism or prayer or treatment or demonstration or meditation or nothingization for the purpose of fixing something that's wrong with the world. Rather you are in the business of realizing that God already is and always has been the only reality anywhere and is right now absolutely, completely and perfectly *present* in full infinite manifestation right here and right now.

Miracles appear to take place when you get a glimmer of that. But the miracles themselves are illusions too. Nothing changed. The broken bone did not change into a whole and perfect bone. It's simply that the totally non-existent illusion of the broken bone was revealed or discovered to be *nothing*. As long as you keep thinking it ever was, it won't disappear. And when you realize that it *never* was, you simply have stopped believing it is possible, you have stopped believing that it *is*. And it is simply because you had been believing that it *is*, that it ever *appeared* in the first place. You are actually creating, moment by moment, the *entire* dream of illusory appearance simply because you continue to believe that something other than God *is*.

The only reason why it seems so hard to let go of that belief is because it has created such a persistent illusion. But again, the illusion *itself* is not persistent; it has no life or ability that would enable it to persist. No, the illusion doesn't persist, but rather you persist in believing the illusion *is*. It simply *isn't*. Simply because God is all there is and all there can be. Simply because God is Truth and anything other than Truth is simply not Truth and simply not so, and therefore simply *isn't*. Any notion of complexity in any of this is also an illusion. God *is*. Nothing else *is*. So all there is, is God being infinitely present right here and right now. There's nothing complex about it at all.

You are not in the business of helping God along with the monumental task of being infinite perfection manifesting infinitely. Rather, you are in the business of relaxing the monumental effort you put forth in trying to be something other than God. God is already infinitely and perfectly present effortlessly. What is your effort all about? What are you endeavoring *against*? Peril? Misfortune? Suffering? Loss? Chaos? Poverty? Loneliness? Illness? Degradation? Entropy? Evil? What are all these things that you work so hard to avoid? Does it make any sense to work hard to avoid *nothing*? And if God is all there is and all there can be, then what can all these things possibly be, but nothing.

Knowing your absolute union with God is effortless. It is believing that you are separate from God that's such a immense task. What could be more monumentally difficult than trying to be something that is impossible? It's impossible for there to be anything other than God, so why keep trying? Why keep pushing and trying? Why? Is it to wake yourself up from the illusion? The illusion has no existence other than your creation of it through your obstinate and effortful clutching to the unintelligible belief that something other than God could be. Why the obstinacy? Why clutch to a belief that is absurd? Is it because you don't completely trust God? Trust God to do what?

You are not in the business of trusting God to protect you from all the bad things that are possible, but rather you are in the business of realizing that God is all there is and therefore "bad things" are impossible. In the end, it's just that simple.

Awareness does not become what it is aware of. It may be aware of itself, but then it simply IS what it is aware of, it doesn't become it. So being aware of a human identity does not make awareness human, any more than being aware of water would make awareness wet. Awareness remains untarnished by anything it ever becomes aware of. But if awareness becomes aware of what IS, it is then aware of itself. When awareness is aware of the presence of God, awareness is being aware of itself. This is absolutely true, but utterly incomprehensible until awareness actually focuses its attention on the presence of God as the only reality. If the momentum of habit is continually inclining you to allow your attention to veer away from God several times a day, then awareness is not focusing its attention on the presence of God as the only reality, and it will be impossible for awareness to be aware of itself as God.

This is also why you cannot *find God* simply by going *inside*. God can't be *inside* if *inside* implies something *outside*. Yes, it's important to block out the dream at intervals and *go deep inside* to meditate. But then when you come out of the meditation you must remain aware only of God's presence everywhere. Otherwise you are simply falling back into the habit of believing in something other than God. If it seems impossible to be aware of God's presence everywhere always, that too is just another habitual response of believing that you yourself are something other than God.

The Truth is, you are totally one and the same infinite being there is no separation between the two of you whatsoever.

The Most Delicate Power of All

Some one comes to you and says, "Heal me, I'm in pain."

Who is this person? This person is the one awareness being all there is, this person is you this *person* is God. It's not just their pain that is the illusion the appearance of being separate from them is an illusion. The Truth is you are totally one and the same infinite being there is no separation between the *two* of you whatsoever.

Where does the illusion of pain come from? It comes from the belief in duality. You cannot view you and *someone else* as someone apart from you and expect their illusion of pain to go away, because the origin of the illusion is the belief that there is anything apart from you. When you realize duality is not true, then you are all there is.

If there is only one, *you* must be that one. Not any beliefs about yourself or any of the illusions about yourself that originate from those beliefs, but the awareness in back and behind those beliefs that remains the same ability to be aware no matter what it is aware of. Your awareness is the *only* thing about you that is all there is. *Everything* else about you is an illusion. You being God's awareness, aware of yourself as infinite awareness is the only thing about you that is all there is. Everything else about you is an illusion.

The appearance of a person separate and apart from you coming to you for help is merely an illusionary echo of your belief in duality. You realize that the appearance of separation between you is absolutely nothing and you see this person as yourself, the one infinite awareness being totally aware of its infinite perfection, God. You simultaneously *intend to see* this and are *receptive to seeing* it at the same time, you simultaneously intend to know God and are receptive to receiving God (the still small voice, the Word of God, the Holy Spirit, *enlightenment, bliss, rapture, ecstasy, illumination, light*) at the same time. You are simultaneously masculine and feminine at the same time. You fuse into one knowing of male and female, being and knowing, existence and awareness, giving and receiving, intending and accepting.

Your male side, so to speak, actively knows the truth: This person is one with me, all there is, is God, and this person and I are one as God, this person and I are the one and the same infinite awareness being all there is, and all appearances to the contrary are nothing whatsoever. At the same time, your feminine side, so to speak, is receptive, open, dilating awareness to *receive* enlightenment. God is the oneness of what the belief in the separateness of masculinity and femininity has split into two. And so within your own self you move towards that oneness, joining back together within yourself what man has put asunder. With every fiber of all your masculine potency you know God is all there is, and at the same time, in exquisitely feminine, delicate and tender openness you relax your emotional armor, you relax your resistances, desires, aversions and fears and allow your awareness to dilate and surrender to being enraptured by God.

But you have to do both at the same time. As long as you experience yourself as something less than God, you have fragmented yourself into male and female, and you experience two dynamics within yourself instead of one. So you will only be supporting the idea of duality if you engage only in one or the other of the two dynamics. You must discover how the two dynamics are in fact *one*. You may start off alternating between the two, thinking/ knowing God is all there is with all your masculine potency, and then feeling/ listening in feminine dilated openness. The Truth is they are not two, but one. So engage in them as one dynamic, rather than as two.

So you simultaneously know and feel the truth about you and this person coming to you for help. If you have to alternate between knowing and feeling the truth for a while that's fine. In actuality, you cannot know the truth without feeling it, nor can you feel the truth without knowing it. What does the oneness of you and the *other* person feel like? Love. What is it that you know about you and this *other* person? Oneness. You really cannot feel love without knowing oneness, nor can you know oneness without feeling love. So you really cannot engage in the masculine dynamic of knowing oneness without at the same time engaging in the feminine dynamic of feeling love. The appearance of the masculine and feminine dynamics being dual is an illusion, a lie about the truth that they are one. So the more you alternate between what starts off as feeling like two different things, knowing the truth and feeling the truth, the more you start to experience them as the *Act of Truth* itself, a oneness of knowing/feeling/loving/being *the most delicate power of all -- God.*

There is no source, other than you, the one, from which anything whatsoever can originate.

Ben Gilberti

Nothingize the Parent

If you are engaged in any kind of endeavoring or efforting of any kind, you always have to ask yourself the question, "What is it that I am trying to achieve?" If you're attempting to achieve it, you must believe you don't already have it, which means you must believe that you are a being other than God. Your belief that you are less than or other than God does not even in the slightest bit inhibit God, the one infinite being that you are now and have always been, the one infinite consciousness that is knowing all there is of infinity, from being always infinitely present everywhere and always and absolutely *as* you and you alone.

God is one. There is no other. God is the only thing there is or can be. You cannot possibly be anything other than God. It is absolutely *impossible* for you to be anything other than God. And your illusions about being less than or other than God have no effect whatever on the reality that you are God, the *only* God, being all, one, whole, perfect, absolute and infinite.

It makes absolutely no difference how long you take to wake up to what you are. When you do wake up the dream won't matter to you one bit. No matter how much you may be mesmerized into believing otherwise, and consequently experiencing otherwise, you still remain the one. *You* still remain the one. Not that other guy, Jesus Christ, or Joel Goldsmith, but you, the one, *in whose infinite consciousness, Joel Goldsmith and Jesus Christ arise.* There is no source, other than you, the one, from which anything whatsoever can originate. All the teaching and wisdom and Divine Grace and Divine Inspiration you receive, can only come from you. Everything you experience originates from you. Any notion otherwise is believing in duality, in the possibility of the existence of something other than God.

Satan would have you believe that it somehow is very good of you to be humble and modest and say, "Oh, me? No, I have a long way to go before I will be fully enlightened and experience myself as God. I'm working towards that, mind you, but rest assured I've still got a long way to go before such a grand attainment." And so here we are, all *Infinite Way* students, almost patting ourselves on our backs for such gracious, self-effacing modesty and humility, "No, not me, I'm still very much mesmerized by that awful *universal mesmerism* that dreadful *mass-consciousness belief in duality* and I don't meditate round that clock like a major mystic and so that mass-consciousness belief in duality sinks into my consciousness all the time and it's going to be a long road of lots of work before the day comes that I will know and experience myself as God." Can't you see what nonsense this is! It *is* the belief in duality.

It poses as something else. It poses as this *wonderful idea* about what your position is in relation to the belief in duality, "It's not really me! You see, it's this other thing, this mass-consciousness belief in duality, that I succumb to like everyone else. See, I'm really very much of a regular guy just like everyone else, poor chaps, all of them victim to that mass-consciousness belief in duality." And so we believe this *wonderful idea* because it appears to be *about* our spiritual development, and *about* how we will ascend up out of our belief in duality. But you see this seeming *wonderful idea* is not *about* your belief in duality, it *is* your belief in duality.

The wonderful idea requires that you believe that something other than God can exist, namely *you*, or, if not you, then something other than you that's making this "Glass darkly that it's so hard for you to see through." You can't believe that there is anything whatsoever that is blocking, inhibiting, darkening, obscuring, limiting, confusing, mesmerizing, or in any other way affecting you being the one God infinitely experiencing yourself as God, and expect to experience yourself as God.

You see, at this point you already know all about how God is all there possibly can be, and that it is the belief in the possibility of the existence of something other than God, which is this belief in duality that is creating all the appearances of suffering and limitation in the dream. You already know all that, and have for some time now. Now you have to apply it to your ideas about spiritual development. As long as you have the idea that your development is going to take time and effort to *attain the realization* that you are God, there is no way you are going to attain that realization, because the idea is the very belief that is creating all the appearance that you think you're somehow stuck with and which appears to validate the belief that it's going to take time and effort.

How can it take time and effort for God to be what God already is? You are God, right now, right this very instant. And you, as God, are right this instant all there is and all there can be. There can't be anything else to inhibit or thwart or darken or becloud or mesmerize or distort or otherwise affect your awareness of yourself as whom and what you really are. It appeared otherwise simply because you believe otherwise. You had belived in duality. You believed that something other than God was possible. But now you know that's ridiculous. You know it is your belief that that which is *not Truth* can be Truth. Truth is all there is -- has to be -- because if there were something else other than Truth, just to be something else other than truth it would of necessity have to be not Truth, and not Truth would have to be so!

It's ridiculous. And yet here we are working hard all day encountering this appearance and that appearance, all of them trying to tempt us into believing in duality while we valiantly try to keep reminding ourselves in countless meditations throughout the day, "No, no, no, God is all there is and all there can be, and so this dreadful appearance can have no reality, etc. etc." ---- all of it because we're happily believing in this *wonderful idea* about spiritual development that presumes that there is something other than the God that you are that is holding you back from experiencing yourself as what you are.

So when you sit down to meditate, before you try to nothingize any other appearance, nothingize this *wonderful idea* about spiritual progress and all the time and effort it's going to take. Nothingize that first. Realize, before you go any further, that the idea that you are <u>not</u> right now as absolutely and completely illumined as God himself, this is <u>not</u> Truth, is <u>not</u> so, and never has been so nor ever will be, and that it was nothing but a completely untrue lie about the Truth that you are right now God in a universe where you, God is all there is and all there ever can be.

To check to see if you have indeed nothingized the *wonderful idea* that there is something other than God inhibiting God from experiencing God as what God is, ask yourself if you expect to get up from this meditation fully illumined. If you don't then you must be believing that it's going to take time and effort to overcome something that is holding you back, something other than God, and maybe in the 3,341st meditation you will arise from your chair fully illumined, but definitely <u>not now</u>, not during *this* meditation so early on in the game. As long as you are believing this what sense is it to be working at nothingizing any other appearance, like pain or suffering or illness or lack or limitation or whatever. All of those other appearances are just the children of the parent belief that there is something inhibiting your full experience of yourself as what you are.

Notice how you spontaneously react with "Wait a minute, here, I can't just give up my belief that I am <u>not</u> already fully illumined!" "I can't just give up my belief that I can't right this instant know everything that God knows and experience everything that God experiences and be everything that God is and have everything that God has and manifest everything that God manifests. I can't do all that in one meditation, for heavens sake! That's asking way, way too much." Notice how natural that belief feels! Notice how comfortable we are with the

35

belief that it all can't happen right now, that it's going to take time. That's the belief to nothingize. The problem wasn't that you weren't very good at nothingizing. The problem was that you were busy nothingizing all these children beliefs while clinging all along to this parent belief that just kept generating more and more of its children. Now nothingize the parent.

Right there where these errors appear, you know with certainty there is only God in perfect peace, splendor, presence and fullness.

From External Forms to Internal Formlessness

You move out of your morning meditation and into your day fully aware of the fact that God is all you are ever going to be and God is all you are ever going to encounter. If dream illusions linger, you are no longer in the least bit perturbed by them. You know that no matter how much of a scene they may display, they have no reality whatever. Right there where these errors appear, you know with certainty there is only God in perfect peace, splendor, presence and fullness.

You may not always see it manifest in the dream world. The dream world may still seem persistent in presenting many "ungodly" appearances. But you do see it in the spiritual world. Your knowledge of the certainty of Truth grows into an internal vision. You may appear to be living at times *between two worlds*, but more and more you begin to see that there is only one world -- God's world -- and that there simply isn't any other world for you to be caught between.

You know, or see inwardly and formlessly that God is 100% present right now. The erroneous appearance on the other hand has some form to it, and appears external to you in some fashion. So you don't see your vision of Truth in form or anything external. Yet each moment of the day your entire approach to living is to always be inwardly looking up from the appearances of external form to the inward, formless, ever present Truth they were lying about. It is vision that is formless and internal, in contrast to the human vision of seeing external form.

You relate to your dream world fully aware that in reality there is only the ecstasy of God here. As a result you leave a trail of miracles you know nothing about. For there is no miracle in nothing remaining nothing. The only reason why the miracles appear to take place is that you got to the place of knowing that the illusion never did have any reality. It is that it always was nothing. You are no longer trying to make the distress disappear. Rather you realize that it's appearance is nothing.

Your priority vision is no longer on the world of appearances. Your priority vision is your vision of Truth. And the more clearly you see, with your inward, formless, spiritual vision, that *God is all there is*, the more clearly you see any appearance to the contrary is therefore absolutely nothing. If the appearances to the contrary continue to appear a while longer, *you see them as a thin mist, a transparent veil, behind which radiates nothing less than God.*

The appearance has nothing to do with your vision of Truth, nothing to do with your certainty of Truth. Rather, the infinite consciousness that you are reveals to you through insight that god really and truly is all there is. And your contemplation of this insight reveals an unfathomable well of feeling. You more and more open yourself up to feel what it feels like to know with certainty that God really and truly is all there is, and as you do so you discover an unfathomable well of peace, equanimity, joy, stillness, gratitude, freedom and love.

Every moment of life you are beholding God with your inward vision and nothingizing anything that appears not to be God. Every moment of your life you are seeing through any ungodly appearances to the Truth the appearances were lying about. The more you do so, the more the world is revealed to be what it only can be and always has been -- the omnipresent, infinite manifestation of God in infinitely perfect Sacred Geometry, the Divine Dance, the Symphony of God.

How could God feel powerless in the face of nothing? How could nothing be an obstacle to you?

Ontological Mysticism   Ben Gilberti

Face the Bullye Eye to Eye

God is our very own being. It's not just that we can reason out to ourselves that Truth is all there can possibly be. God is our very own being. The infinite, perfect manifestation of infinite consciousness is our very own being. Yet we say, "I know God is all that I can be, but I am not yet enlightened, I am not experiencing myself as God."

What do we do about that? Do we work harder at spiritual studies and disciplines so that we can fix the problem of not experiencing ourselves as God? Unquestionably we all do. What is all that study and discipline trying to get us to realize? Isn't it that any experience other than God is nothing, and should be treated as nothing?

Any experience we have of ourselves appearing to be less than or other than God should be treated as what it is -- nothing -- and worthy of no attention whatsoever. What then do we turn our attention towards? What's left? *I being God.* "But I don't experience myself as being God." Well, the experience is nothing, so why are you putting attention to it?

"I can't help it, I can't climb out of it, I feel like I'm stuck inside of it." Well, OK, but is that an experience of Truth or an experience of a lie about Truth? And what is the Truth that it is a lie about? *I being God.*

"Yes, I know that I being God is the Truth, and that anything else is not the Truth and not so, I know that, but I still don't experience myself as God." What makes you say that? Whatever it is, you already know it is an illusion, you already know it is not of God and has no life or reality whatsoever, you already know it is a phantom resting on nothing you already know it IS nothing, in contrast to which you already know you are God. No matter how vivid your experience of the illusion may be, there clearly cannot be any doubt that is an illusion. You already know illusion is nothing and is <u>no</u> match for you whom you already know is God.

In-other-words, so what if you experience yourself as less than or other than God. So what!? You already know that the experience is an illusion that is nothing, and that nothing is hardly anything of any consequence to God. So what if you experience yourself as less than God?! It certainly isn't anything to feel powerless in the face of! After all it is nothing, and you are God! How could God feel powerless in the face of nothing? How could nothing be an obstacle to you?

Don't let it bully you. It's nothing. Turn right around and face the bully eye to eye. Answer the question, "What's giving me the impression that I am less than or other than God?" Make a list. And then nothingize each item on the list. You've put a lot of hard work into creating those impressions, and you are right now trussing them up in place with effort. They're not standing up by virtue of any other effort but your own anyway, so all you have to do is get your reality thinking up enough to prove they're nothing and the effort that's been trussing them up (your own) will collapse, and with it the impression it was creating the illusion of. Then you'll be left alone with what you already are -- God.

If you find that you aren't left all alone with yourself (God), but that there are yet still other impressions remaining of being less than God, well, so what!? They aren't real either. When you feel like it, make a list of them too, and pull the rug out from under them as well.

You rise to live as the Son of God, One with God, in a world consisting only of God manifesting limitlessly.

Ben Gilberti

The Divine Flower

The principle of God being all there is, is not fully comprehended until every last appearance to the contrary is nothingized. Every time you nothingize an appearance you see through it to yet another manifestation of God, complete in itself, and in the most intimate resonance with the infinity of God's manifestation. Multiplicity of appearances ultimately nothingize to reveal infinity where multiplicity appeared.

We actually begin to see God manifesting in our lives. All that is going on in the first place, of course, is that God and God alone is manifesting in our lives infinitely. But as we apply that principle to nothingize the appearances, those appearances dissolve to reveal the Truth they were a lie about. Yes, it is the same truth we started off with, but there is a deeper revelation of what consciousness experiences when it knows it is the one and only infinitely manifesting God.

Each healing or miracle is a revelation of God's manifestation. All that a miracle is, is a revelation of another attribute of God's infinite manifestation, not only in insight, but also in the elevation of the quality of the flow of one's life as it moves more in alignment and harmony with the attribute newly revealed. You're life feels like its becoming symphonic. Extraordinary coincidences chime perfectly in place. Every encounter is the perfect encounter and ripe with the most extraordinary of all opportunities -- the opportunity to nothingize yet another mass-consciousness belief contrary to the nature of God and as a consequence reveal the manifestation of attributes of God that were previously hidden. As you leave your wake of miracles, you feel yourself being the manifestation of God, the manifestation of Grace. As you flow into being one note in the divine symphony you find yourself feeling a more intimate union with the entire symphony. You have a glimmer already that if you were to live totally by grace and inspiration alone, you would feel the most intimate union with God and all God's manifestation.

In a way it surprises you. You still do what you used to do. You might refine it a little, but basically you still do what you were doing. The difference is that it is no longer important. The only thing that is important to you now is nothingizing appearances so that God can be more fully revealed.

You still talk about the latest movies or politics or cooking or whatever, you still work and play, but now you're wide open to God manifesting. And almost to your surprise God does manifest, right there in your life, in countless thousands of subtle, exquisite, gracious and liberating ways. It wouldn't matter to you whether you were a housekeeper or a movie star. Your important business would be just the same -- to nothingize appearances so that God can be more fully revealed. And you find that you really like the work. You're delighted to discover that it is incomparably better than any other job you've had before. Inspiration begins to lead you to a continual discovery of your part in the divine symphony. You feel completely at home. You know your purpose and mission in life and are living it.

A resurrection takes place. You rise from the tomb of the mass consciousness belief in duality. You rise up out of the tomb of fear, worry, anxiety, peril, stress, lack, weakness, grief, terror, pain, suffering, guilt, confusion, alienation, loneliness, frustration, irritation, and all the other lies about God's attributes. You rise to live as the Son of God, One with God, in a world consisting only of God manifesting limitlessly. Your life becomes the great adventure of discovering the limitlessness of God.

It doesn't even matter to you anymore what appearances present them to you for nothingization. Any appearance, great or small, is another opportunity to discover yet even more of God's limitlessness. And after a while, others will come to you, offering you their appearances for you to nothingize. And it's all fine by you. As far as you're concerned, there isn't anything better to do than to reveal more of God's limitlessness.

You nothingize both the assumed and projected aspects of the appearance as two sides of the same lie, and both sides, both you and your world dilate further into God's limitlessness. Your whole life becomes dilation an opening up, a blossoming, and an unfolding.......a flower.

To identify with your True Self, to know that your consciousness is identical with God, is to experience absolute ecstasy and peace.

Death and Ecstasy

ecstasy (èk¹ste-sê) noun

1.   Intense joy or delight.
2.   A state of emotion so intense that one is carried beyond rational thought and self-control.
3.   The trance, frenzy, or rapture associated with mystic or prophetic exaltation.

Synonyms: ecstasy, rapture. These nouns refer to a state of elated bliss. In its original sense ecstasy denoted a trancelike condition marked by loss of orientation toward rational experience and by concentration on a single emotion; now it usually means intense delight: *"To burn always with this hard, gemlike flame, to maintain this ecstasy, is success in life"* (Walter Pater). Rapture originally meant a being caught up in an emotional state, typically involuntary and uncontrollable. In current usage rapture, like ecstasy, simply means great joy*: "Oliver would sit . . . listening to the sweet music, in a perfect rapture"* (Charles Dickens).

You must be continually asking your youreself, "Who is it that is endeavoring to develop spiritually?" And each time we become aware of that identity, nothingize it. God would not make an effort to expand spiritually. To be working at spiritual development means that you are identifying as a being other than God, identifying as something that is a lie about the Truth that God is all there is and all that you can be. The fact that you are identifying as something that is nothing is nothing to be concerned or worried about in the least, because it is nothing. To free ourselves from the illusion of thinking it isn't nothing, we set out as beings identifying as something that is nothing, and out of yearning for a real self we think we lost, we embark on spiritual development, and we learn to nothingize appearances of nothing pretending to be something.

That's the endeavor. Now we also realize that the endeavourer himself must be seen through to the Truth he is a lie about. This is how we die daily. We also rise daily from the tomb of what we nothingized to a fuller manifestation of the Truth that we are. The nature of the appearances presenting themselves to us for nothingization doesn't matter to us very much at all. Now what matters, is *who* we are discovering ourselves to be as the onion layers of false identity fall away. Now what matters is *how* we relate to all appearances in general, rather than what those appearances may at any moment involve. It isn't what happens to us that matters now, but what we do in response, and who it is that is making such a response.

Your identity becomes a blossoming flower. It is evermore always opening up to God. Dilating to be filled with God and surrendering into a fusion with God. It is ecstasy with no limits. It is the ecstasy of all there is being in ecstasy. And it also is absolute stillness.

Nothingization is the Truth that destruction is a lie about. Rather than destroy that which distresses us, we instead nothingize our belief that it is anything distressing, and see it as God "writhing in ecstasy at our feet." Our original motivation to nothingize something, the intention to annihilate something bad, annihilates instead our belief that anything bad is possible.

The self that can see anything bad, dies. The self that only can see God, rises. And there, to our newborn astonished self is God writhing in ecstasy, there, right were we once thought there was something bad. And yet all of it happens in absolute stillness and tranquillity. The mundanities of life continue without the slightest ripple of disturbance, except for the sweet smell of a flower, and the serenity of peace. To *identify* with your True Self, to know that your consciousness is *identical* with God, is to experience absolute ecstasy and peace. It is to know that nothing can die but that which never was. It is to embrace the whole world as your beloved. It is to feel the joy of both you and your beloved writhing in the ecstasy of your love, your fusion, your oneness. It is to know that you are all life, and that all life flows through you:

Awareness can never be presented with something to be aware of that comes from outside itself. It can only be aware of its own, one, infinite, self.

Ben Gilberti

All There is, is You

Awareness being aware of itself only, is the key. Awareness is. There is no doubt about that. And what is, is one, besides which there is no other. Satan is the belief that there is another. That's when you have duality and all that duality generates (suffering, pain, fear, death, disease, malice, etc., etc., etc., etc). It all originates from the belief that awareness can be aware of anything but itself. That's the big lie that is the father of all lies (the Devil). It is simply the belief that awareness can be aware of anything but itself.

Awareness can never be presented with something to be aware of that comes from outside itself. It can only be aware of its own, one, infinite, self, because there is no other. Truth is all there is besides which there can not be anything else. God is all there is besides which there is no other. And so it must be that Awareness is all there is, besides which there is nothing else. So awareness is always being aware simply of itself.

All the distress comes from awareness judging something that it is aware of as alien or originating from some other source other than itself. Once the *I* realizes that *I* created it all, then nothing any longer can be a threat, because you were creating it all along, just for the purpose of feeling what it would feel like if you were limited, instead of infinite, fragmented, instead of one, insignificant, instead of absolute, boxed in, instead of free, unknowing, instead of omniscient, a tiny speck, instead of omnipresent, powerless, instead of omnipotent. You remain all along the one, infinite, absolute, free, omniscient, omnipresent, omnipotent awareness, and it is you who are creating the illusion of limitation, simply to feel what it would feel like, for no other reason.

You are <u>not</u> in the slightest bit stuck in the illusion. You are creating it every moment. And you can stop creating it at any moment. Simply by becoming aware of awareness and realizing that all that you are aware of is also your awareness too. Don't judge what you experience, or what you see. Either it's God in manifestation or it's an illusion of something other than God. In either case it is totally harmless.

 If it's an illusion, it's still only an illusion created by you in your own awareness, having no other life, and no other source, but you. If you want to nothingize it, simply stop creating your belief in it, and it will disappear, because it isn't there anyway. All it is, is reflection of your belief in it, your belief that it is something other than you. You are awareness, and awareness is all there is, so there is nothing other than you. It's only the idea that there is that creates all the problems.

So when you greet any experience, or view anything you see, as simply you, you have solved the problem. All the "yes, but" and "but what ifs" merely come from the same problem perspective that there can be something other than you. If it's you, it can't harm you, because you are awareness, and awareness is one.

It is the Devil who suggests the Satanic idea. The Satanic idea is: You are <u>not</u> the only one, there is another. Your awareness is <u>not</u> the sole awareness, there is another. Your being is <u>not</u> the only being, there is another. From that idea comes all the other ideas that create illusory problems: God is another being besides you, and you are something other than God. The world is something else besides you, and something else besides God, too.

The solution to all these Satanic ideas is one thing and one thing alone -- The Christ -- who says, "Be still, and know that I am God." The Christ in You, the *I*, does not say this to the illusions; it does not tell the illusions to be still as though they were doing anything of their own. The Christ in you, your awareness, says this to the sense of self that is creating the illusions by believing they are possible, to that self, <u>not</u> to the illusions, your awareness says, "Be still and know that I am God." "Be still, I only pretended to be you to feel what it feels like, I am your source, so Be still," your awareness says, "It is I who am God, God is what I am."

I am absolutely free. It is a realization that releases me from all fear. I am absolutely safe. It is a realization that releases me from all want. I am absolutely all, infinitely.

In God's Heaven
(contemplative meditation)

God is all there is. Be still and know that I am God. Anything else I experience about myself is nothing. I do not have to make amends for it. I do not have to overcome it. I do not even have to confront it! There is nothing to confront, overcome or make amends for. All there is, is God. That's all. All my sins and guilt were but a dream about nothing. There are no mistakes for which I have to pay. There is nothing for which I need to be forgiven. All of that was just part of the dream of duality, the dream of nothing. And I can completely let go of the entire dream right now by simply turning the focus of my awareness away from the dream and towards the reality of what I already am and always have been and always will be, God.

I will just be still and know that I am God. I ignore, for the moment, anything else I experience about myself. I will not get busy right away trying to nothingize any of that, not just yet. For the moment I turn my attention entirely towards my awareness of being awareness being aware that this awareness alone is the I that I am that is God and that is all there is. I contemplate on the fact that it is my own awareness that is the God towards which I have been reaching all this time.

I contemplate *my awareness itself is God.* If I am

aware of being one and infinite and perfect and absolute as I in fact am, if I am aware of that, then that is what I experience. My awareness itself is God. If I chose to make believe that anything other than God is possible, then that is what I experience by reason of my- make-believe. My awareness itself is God. All my problems are illusions that I and I alone have made from my own beliefs.

My awareness itself is God. With my awareness now aware of itself as God, I know that I am everything that God is, and everything there is, is the God that I am. I have no interest whatever in anything that appears otherwise. I have no interest in illusions. I know that I am the one God knowing and being all there is. I am in the dream but not of it. The dream means absolutely nothing to me whatsoever. Anything other than God being God is of no interest to me at all. All I do is see right through all dream appearances all the time. It isn't the dream I am interested in seeing, it's God being God that commands all my attention.

I already know that there in fact is nothing else to put one's attention to. To put my attention to a dream of something other than God is to put my attention to nothing. I have no interest in nothing. All my interest and attention is focused on the only thing there is, God being God. All of my attention is focused on one thing and one thing alone, that right this instant and in every instant always, all that's going on is that God is being God. Nothing else whatsoever is ever happening! I have no interest in any appearance of something else going on. Nothing else is going on. What do I care that I appear to be in a world where 99% believe that something other than God is possible. I know that's part of the dream illusion too. I know there is nothing but God being God, here, now, and always. I am in total peace and ecstasy at each and every moment of my life. I know who I am. I am the one God who is absolutely all there is, the one God who is entire, total, complete, perfect, absolute and infinite. I am that.

I am not interested in a dream that appears otherwise. I instantly see right through any and all dreams that appear otherwise. I am in the dream but not of it. I'm always in the dream seeing right through it to what is really going on -- God being God. I live each moment in this realization. And I am at peace within this realization. There isn't anything I need to prove within the dream. It is a realization that releases me from all obligations. I am absolutely free. It is a realization that releases me from all fear. I am absolutely safe. It is a realization that releases me from all want. I am absolutely all, infinitely.

From this springs all my delight, just as radiantly when I'm making coffee as when I'm healing someone at their request. I gladly do anything that the dream drama appears to require of me, not from any sense of obligation, but purely of my own free choice. Because in contrast to what I know my self to really be, God being all there is. There is nothing within the dream drama that could possibly be of any interest to me one way or another. Roles of any kind in the dream drama, other than God being God, I know are nothing. Whatever role I discover myself in the middle of as I awaken as I have now to the realization that all roles other than God being God are nothing, is of no consequence to me at all. All that matters to me is that I am God being God, and that God being God is all that is ever happening.

Whatever a biographer might write about my life up to this point is of no consequence whatsoever. No matter whether that biographer would speak of my greatness or my infamy, makes absolutely no difference whatsoever. None of it ever had any reality at all. All there ever was, or is, or will be is God being God, and that is what I am now.

This is the source of all my delight, whether I'm sweeping the floor or inspiring a loved one to tears of bliss. I know that I am always, in every moment of life, doing nothing else but making love to myself. I am all there is. All there is, is what I am. And being one with all there is, is what love is. God is perfect love and God is what I am. Everything I do, no matter what I do, is I making love to myself.

How much does God appreciate himself? That is how much I appreciate myself, God, who I am, and who I meet every moment of every day in anything and everything I ever do. Why would I have even the slightest, tiniest interest in being fooled by any dream appearance to the contrary?! I am *in* the dream, but not in the slightest degree *of* it. I am *of* my own self -- God. And that is the sole source of my limitless delight. My awareness that God being God is all that is ever happening is the sole source of all my delight.

My awareness itself is God being God. If I chose to be aware of God being God only, that is the only thing I will be aware of. I now know that God being God is all there is and all that ever can be happening ever. Appearances to the contrary can no longer get me to believe in the beliefs that create them. Appearances to the contrary are now like a fading echo of something I now realize was nothing. The former passes away and is no longer brought to mind. I am God, and God is too pure to behold iniquity. I pay no attention to the fading echo of nothing.

I delight in seeing God only, right here where the fading echo still lingers. I take great delight in knowing that the dream illusion is nothing. I take great delight in knowing that the dream doesn't matter at all. I take great delight in knowing that all that matters is that I am God. I take great delight in knowing that the contemplation of myself as God, the loving of myself as God in every thing that I do in every moment of my life is unfolding itself in an infinitely expanding revelation of my own inexpressibly exquisite infinity. Practicing the Presence of God is for me infinitely more delightful than anything the dream drama holds out as providing delight. I'm always enjoying the presence of God.

I am at every moment in God's Heaven.

Until the idea of the devil is nothingized, you are necessarily stuck with the experience of being the devil.

Ontological Mysticism   Ben Gilberti

The Spiritual Application

of E=mc2

When Einstein discovered $E=mc^2$, he discovered a law, a principle that entire universe obeys. Because we believe the universe is physical, we have so far only applied the law to what we experience as the physical universe. But it is possible to apply the same principle to what we know the universe is really made of -- consciousness.

The principle $E=mc^2$ states that anything which resists movement, any inertia, anything that requires energy to move it, can itself be transformed into the very ability needed to move it -- energy, and that the transformation of inertia into energy occurs when two opposites fuse. When an anti-proton collides and fuses with a proton, the mass or inertia of both bodies completely disappears in a burst of pure energy.

Now pure energy is different from kinetic energy. Kinetic energy is the energy of bodies of mass as they move relative to each other. Pure energy, on the other hand, is electro-magnetic vibration, having no mass or inertia whatsoever, and always in movement at one constant speed, the speed of light.

Keep in mind that this entire phenomenon can have no existence whatsoever except within your consciousness, inasmuch as there cannot be any separation from your consciousness and God's. And so the entire phenomenon is actually about the dynamics with which consciousness creates the illusion of the physical universe, the universe of inertia and energy, the universe of duality. There is no physical universe without the duality of inertia and energy. Energy is that which can move that which resists movement.

Inertia is resistance to energy's ability to move it, absorbing energy's ability to move that which resists movement by converting energy into inertial movement. Inertial movement is altogether different from the movement of the speed of light. Light is always moving at the maximum speed the physical universe permits, and offers no resistance whatsoever in any change in the direction in which it is going.

Inertial movement, on the other hand, could never move as fast as light even if it were the tiniest body of mass in the universe, an electron, and if all the energy in the universe were to be applied to its acceleration. It would never reach the speed of light. In the process of approaching the speed of light it would acquire more and more mass, become heavier and heavier. Continuing until, when it had absorbed all the energy of the whole universe, it would become itself just as massive as the whole universe was before it converted itself into energy to move this one little electron.

It's is a little awesome to consider that this entire phenomenon occurs only in your consciousness! Nevertheless, so it does. So you can apply the principle of nuclear energy to your own consciousness. Just take the two opposites postulated by the theory of duality and fuse them and wham they will annihilate into pure energy just like they do at Fermilab. The very thing that resists your movement towards spiritual enlightenment can itself be converted into the spiritual energy to catapult you to full realization. Does that sound amazing? It should it is just as amazing as the Hydrogen Bomb.

Let's take the opposites of pleasure and pain. Guilt is expectation of punishment or pain. Guilt is created out of our belief in duality. Pleasure must have its opposite -- pain. And why, in a world created and sustained by God, would the experience of pain emerge? To pay for your evil and for your devilishness in saying to yourself, "I will knock God off his throne and be God in his place." To whom does the word devil refer? Does it refer to a being outside of you? You know better now than to believe that anymore. So to whom then does the word devil refer? To you, of course.

Until the idea of the devil is nothingized, you are necessarily stuck with the experience of being the devil. Oh, you may project it out on to other beings out there, but that's just your way of trying to deny what you fear you have done. You are the only one, remember. You are God. There is nothing else in the entire universe but you. Whether you experience yourself this way yet or not, you still remain The one and only God being all.

The horror and its resolution intersect, like matter and anti-matter, and burst into pure energy, pure consciousness. What is the ultimate horror? It is that you discover that you are the devil. Notice the faint whiff of terror that the very idea evokes! And what is its resolution? Simplicity itself, God is all. There is no devil and never was. The entire idea of the existence of something opposed to God is absolutely impossible. God is always all there is and always has been.

There is no such thing as enmity against God that St. Paul believed in so seriously, and suffered such torture as a result. It was only the idea that there could be something opposed to God that created all the illusion of suffering. An idea that justifies suffering as deserved punishment for having committed the most heinous crime of all infamy -- being opposed to God.

And what is the opposite of pain? Pleasure! And therefore the enjoyment of pleasure is construed to be somehow in opposition to God. Oh, civilized pleasures, are ok. The subdued and decorous pleasures of art and music, and even fine cuisine, are ok. But engage in pleasure that drives you out of your mind with rapture and ecstasy and the idea does its best to create scenarios of guilt. And yet enlightenment is a totally ecstatic experience. God feels only bliss. The greatest pleasure of all would be to be God. Not one mystic who ever wrote of their own enlightenment ever speaks of it except in terms of ecstasy. So naturally, the belief in duality must insist that ecstasy is evil.

This is the ugly underbelly of the dream illusion that everyone runs from. Wilhelm Reich came close to it and died in prison for having done so. He called it the *Emotional Plague*. Emotion comes from a Latin root that means ability to move -- the same meaning as the word energy. We can no longer take a British position, snubbing our nose at the ugly emotions in a posture that claims to have transcended the underbelly before we have even admitted it.

We must get to the root and confront the underbelly, see the horrible illusion of the devil as our own creation. Only then can we nothingize it. If we think it has its origin outside of us then we still believe in duality, and duality is what we will experience. You must realize that the idea of evil exists only in your awareness and no where else. All awareness is your awareness. The idea of the devil can't come from anywhere else but from you, because you are all there is.

The horror and its resolution intersect and annihilate into pure energy, pure consciousness. As you look directly at the horror of all horrors: All the evil in the whole world originated entirely and only from me! At that same instant you are realizing that you are God being all there is besides which there is nothing else.

The horror and its resolution annihilate (nothingize) in a nuclear explosion of pure energy, pure consciousness. That which is left is the Divine Consciousness that knows *I am God being all, entire, total, complete, perfect, absolute, infinite, one, harmonious, pure, free, limitless, bliss, and besides me there is no other*.

God does not know good and evil. The original temptation was to be as gods, knowing good and evil. Once you know good and evil, you have identified yourself as something other than God. The price you have to pay for identifying as a being who can know good and evil is that you have to be that evil that you know. If you identify as God, you cannot know good and evil. If you identify as someone who knows good

69

and evil, you are necessarily identifying as that which is other than God, that which is <u>not</u> God, that which is not whole, complete, perfect and infinite, that which is fragmented, incomplete, flawed and limited; you have identified as the very evil you must necessarily postulate as possible in order for you to know good and evil. And we become, not God, but *as gods*. We are the prodigal son having left the Father. We have left paradise for hell, the world wherein the devil rules. The devil who would knock God off his throne and create his own universe in place of God's.

God's universe is absolute and perfect and is never anything else. The devil, that identity that presumes it is <u>not</u> God but something apart from God. This devil asserts its presumption by creating a universe other than God's universe, a universe that is a sea of limitation and imperfection.

How could one pay for such a crime? If it were possible to commit such a crime and succeed, the devil will have murdered God. If such a thing were possible, how could one pay for such a crime? It would be impossible. God would be dead. All would be lost forever. Horror and terror and dreadful pain would be all there is forever. It would be impossible. And for this reason all the orthodox and mainstream "Christian" denominations claim that the devil will be eventually thrown into a lake of fire to suffer forever, and God will be triumphant and in supreme bliss while all the while knowing that there remains in the universe a horrific consciousness that is now suffering the horrible torture it will deserve for all eternity.

Look at how utterly insane is what man has thought

up about God's creation! And yet we apply that same insanity, in a far more reduced version, into our everyday lives, as though a mild version of insanity is any less insane. We continue to believe that we are somewhat, but not altogether apart from God, and that we create a reality that is "somewhat, but not entirely other than God's universe, and we condemn ourselves to suffering we thereby believe we deserve, suffering that is somewhat, but not entirely like hell.

The only resolution to evil, as long as evil is considered to have any reality whatsoever, is the insane resolution of hell. And the only resolution to such insanity is one thing and one thing only, and that is the realization that there is <u>no</u> such thing as evil, <u>no</u> such thing as disharmony, imperfection, incompleteness, isolation, separation, death, disease, or suffering of any kind. There is <u>no</u> such thing as opposition to God of any kind, <u>no</u> such thing as *being apart from God*. And your nightmare that it was possible was nothing but a dream, it never happened, it never will happen, and there exists nowhere anyone who is responsible for making it happen or who has to pay for the crime of having done it. There is no such thing as righteous condemnation. There is only insane self-condemnation. And there is only one Truth the insanity lies about -- You are now and have always been pristine, and purely innocent.

When you think to yourself, if I accept that idea, it may grant me license to do evil with no conscience. -- Who is thinking that idea? Would God think such an idea? Would God be reluctant to accept His own absolute purity and innocence lest he lose a conscience that holds him back from committing evil? Nothing of course not. Notice how we cling to the idea that we cannot be as pure and as innocent as God! And notice how we cling to that idea with the notion that it keeps us more sure-footed on our spiritual journey! It's the very thing that slows down our spiritual journey! It's the one thing that resists movement along our spiritual journey. It is our spiritual inertia.

We've been pushing against it with energy derived elsewhere. In the physical world we endeavored to overcome physical inertia by finding the energy to do so from some other place than the very thing that was resisting movement until. Einstein came along and explained that the resistance to movement itself could be transformed into the ability to move. Don't push against it. That only fortifies the notion that reality is not one. The idea that there can be something to push against only fortifies the notion of duality. Transform it instead. Your spiritual inertia is your belief that you are not as absolutely innocent and pure as God. Nothingize it. Annihilate it. Admit that all evil everywhere is your own insane presumption. Let that presumption collide with your realization that only God can ever be. And watch all your guilt, self-condemnation and fear dissolve into pure energy, infinite movement, instantaneous omnipresence, infinite perfection, absolute innocence, crystalline purity.

And so it is that we often conceive of the path to enlightenment as something requiring epic proportions of heroic effort, concentration and discipline. None of it has the slightest thing to do with the nature of spirit.

The Hallucinations of Duality

Failure, it would seem, would be to have spent most of one's life running away from the pains, and running towards the pleasures, which constitute the fabric of the universe of duality --- in other words, to live a life enmeshed in the fabric of duality, to have poured your time and energy into all manner of devices to protect you from pain and increase your pleasure.

The duality is not between God and what is <u>not</u> God. That which is not God, has no existence. The duality is between good and evil, pleasure and pain. *To evaluate anything as good or evil is to do that which creates the illusion of something other than God.* But that something is the good/evil duality itself, not just one side of it. That which is appearing as a universe that it less than God, is not just the evil in the world, but also the opposites of that evil. That which is appearing as a universe that is less than God, appears that way only because we have been evaluating everything as good or evil. It's the belief in duality, the belief that the universe is good and evil, and we have to figure out what part is good and get as much of it as possible, and we have figure out which part is bad and avoid it as much as possible.

It is an insult to God to presume that a universe he created is split into good and evil. Then we become as gods, because God himself didn't get it all right, and we are the ones now who are going to do a better job than God did. We will try to do this by destroying, or at least ostracizing the half of his creation that is evil and arranging to acquire as much of his creation that is good.

It isn't that the good things are divine and the evil things illusory appearances. God is not all that we have labeled good excluding all that we have labeled bad. We're not in the business of nothingizing all the bad stuff so that we're left only with the good-- and to the extent we are we find nothingization a never-ending chore. We're in the business of nothingizing the entire good-bad illusion so that we're left only with God.

And we cannot nothingize the bad and the good separately as though they were, as they appear to be, two separate things. Good and evil are the same thing -- the hallucination of duality. The belief that there is good and evil is what must be nothingized, not the good things or the bad things that arise from that belief. Our labeling *everything good or evil is the source of the illusion*, the illusion of a world half of which we desire and the other half of which we resist with aversion. And so, living a life pursing desires and avoiding aversions is, it would seem, to be a failure.

And success, it would seem, would be to be living the life of Grace. Living a life where God is your supply, not money; where love is your motivation, not greed or hunger for power; where inspiration and intuition is your guidance, not crafty scheming; where peace is your feeling, not turbulent emotional reactivity to all your duality evaluations. A life where God is your being, not a limited and vulnerable self who has to scurry to get good and avoid bad. Such would seem to be spiritual success, for indeed it would indicate having avoided spiritual failure. Notice the duality again! We now have just gone ahead and applied our belief in duality to the spiritual world! We are now reaching for holiness and avoiding wickedness!

Spiritual wickedness is man's idea of the attempt to use intellectual concepts about spiritual principles in order to achieve greater success in the duality game. Spiritual holiness is man's idea of what's involved in the immersion of oneself in the spiritual principle that only God is. But both wickedness and holiness must also be seen to be two sides of the same coin -- another instance of the belief in duality. Whereas good and evil were general terms, holiness and wickedness represent the application of our belief in duality to the spiritual world. We presume the spiritual world is dual just like anything else, and so we get busy labeling this wicked and that holy, and then of course we have to become very busy avoiding the wicked and pursuing the holy. Our belief in duality makes us slaves of duality. Our belief in duality becomes a relentless taskmaster, whipping us continually to make a greater effort to pursue good, and avoid evil. And when we first enter the spiritual path we inadvertently enslave ourselves to our dualistic version of spirit. We work hard at self examination and spiritual study and countless meditations and seminars and tapes and books and writings and conversations --- all of it in an effort to attain more God and eliminate more hypnotism. We don't realize that in doing so we are acting out our having hypnotized ourselves into enslavement to our dualistic version of spirit. We would always be straining to attain more of a realization of God and we would always be having to become ever more and more vigilant, alert and skilled at more and more elegant techniques for nothingizing the unending parade of appearances that would inevitably issue from our premise that spirit is dual.

And so it is that we often conceive of the path to enlightenment as something requiring epic proportions of heroic effort, concentration and discipline. None of it has the slightest thing to do with the nature of spirit. All of it is itself the illusory appearance of our having hypnotized ourselves into believing that the world of spirit is also dual, and so we have to work just as hard to make sure we don't end up on the wrong side of spiritual duality, just as much as we had to work hard to make sure we didn't end up on the wrong side of physical duality when we used to think that the world was material.

The solution, of course, is to nothingize the entire notion of spiritual duality by realizing that being God is not a project to be achieved with heroic execution of a carefully designed strategic plan. There are no perilous consequences to imagining that God is _not_ all there is, both for one absolutely simple reason, simply because God is all there is. There is not God and the glorious execution of the path to attainment of God. There is not God and that zenith of vigilant and disciplined attention that avoids the consequences of imagining that God is not all there is by rigorously avoiding any thought of such a thing. All of that is just hypnotism, and hypnotism is nothing.

All there is, is just God. God is all. Hypnotism is nothing. That's all you need to know. Nothing else. God is all. Hypnotism is nothing. As you contemplate that you begin to realize it. As you begin to realize it, you begin to relax all the anxiety, worry, confusion, fear, resistance, urgency, lust, need, guilt and all the other turbulence stirred up by the belief in duality. You begin to rest in God. You begin to be in peace. And that's when you begin to feel what it feels like to be in a universe consisting only of God. Moses leads us away from the slave-driver, Pharos, the belief in duality. Moses leads you away from the turbulence of duality. It is in the peace that remains that you enter the Promised Land, without Moses. Why without Moses? Because, Moses disappears too, Moses was part of the hypnosis. There isn't God and a spiritualized intellect that leads you out of the dream of duality. There is just God. Nothing else, just God. One.

Duality is not the opposite of oneness. Believing that duality is the opposite of oneness is just the belief in duality all over again. But here is where the buck stops. Duality is not the opposite of oneness because duality isn't. Only oneness is. Duality isn't evil and oneness isn't good. Duality isn't wicked and oneness holy. Oneness simply is. And duality simply isn't.

I know there is only God, and hence there is no lack, there is no evil, there is no resistance, there is no injury, no disease, no limitation.

Self-Confrontation

Who chooses to be something other than God? To whatever extent you experience yourself as something other than God, you do. And who are you to make such a choice? Is it not a sense of self that *feels like* it is less than God? Does that sense of self have any power or reality to it? You already know it can't because God is all there is. And if God is all there is, then what is this appearance of something other than God? You already know it is hypnotism from the belief in duality.

The hypnotism that comes out of the belief in duality manifests itself, in this case, in your being hypnotized. Hypnotized into an experience, a sense of self that will prove that the belief in duality is true. It does this by creating the hallucination of experiencing yourself as something apart, or dual, in its relationship with God. That false sense of self appears just as vividly as the swarm of snakes you'd see in place of a Christmas tree if you were hypnotized to believe that the tree was a swarm of snakes. Nothing the snakes do has any power or reality. There are no snakes there at all. Neither is there your limited sense of self. *It simply isn't there.* All you're experiencing is a hypnotic hallucination.

Dehypnotize yourself from the belief in duality and the hallucination disappears. The hallucination in this case is your own limited sense of self. You dehypnotize yourself by confronting this limited sense of self and calling its bluff.

Say to the appearance, "You are showing to me another way in which I believe in duality and hypnotize myself into experiencing a universe at war with itself. By showing this to me you are contributing to my awakening and the great awakening of all humanity. You are part of my unfoldment. This appearance that you are, this limited sense of self I feel myself to be, is simply another way in which I believe in duality. It is my belief in duality as it pertains to my own self. Because I believed in duality, my own self had to be experienced as dual, in conflict with itself, limiting and opposing itself, at war with itself, at war with the world, and at war with God. All of it was nothing but the hallucination of the kind of self I'd be if the belief in duality were true. But I know now that the belief in duality is not true. Nothing else can be but that which is. God is. There can be no other than God being. And hence there is no other with which to be in conflict or at war. God is. I am. I am what God is. God is what I am. There can be no other. There is only one being, God, I, consciousness."

Continue to address the appearance until its bluff is completely exposed:
"I know there is only God, and hence there is nothing to fear. I know there is only God, and hence there is nothing with which, or about which, to be in conflict. I know there is only God, and hence there is no lack, there is no evil, there is no resistance, there is no injury, no disease, no limitation. You, my dear appearance, are nothing but Satan's face. Satan's heart is the belief

in duality, and you, merely an appearance of that belief, Satan's face. And so I have only one thing to say to you, appearance, and that is, 'Get thee behind me, Satan.' I do not accept what you are suggesting. There is nothing other than God. I know that is the Truth. And you, appearance, face of Satan, are suggesting otherwise. You are a liar and I do not believe you. I don't care how bold-faced you are about lying, I don't care what a vivid appearance you make, you are lying just the same. So get thee behind me. Your suggestion that there can be something other than God is simply not true. There is nothing other than God. And hence all that I can be is God."

Say all that to the appearance. Explain to the appearance how and why it is a lie, not true, not so, nothing. *As you do so, your reactivity to the appearance will disappear, because it was only because you believed the appearance was true that you were reacting to it in the first place.* It's much like the reactivity you might have in response to a mirage of water in the desert if you didn't know it was a mirage. You might react by getting upset about how a lake of water was now blocking your path and may get all worked up trying to figure out ways to drive around the lake. Once you realize that the lake of water is only a mirage, you drive right into it without the slightest concern, having no reaction to it whatsoever, and sure enough it gradually disappears. So you will be at peace even while the appearance continues to appear because you are not reactive to the appearance anymore. It may still be there for a little while, but you now know that it is only a hallucination, a suggestion to believe something that is not true. You now know it is nothing. And so even while the appearance lingers, a little while, it has no

83

effect on you. You are no longer reacting to it in any way.

It was your reactivity, you see, that was getting you all riled up. It was your reactivity that was disturbing your peace. And now that the reactivity is gone, you are at peace again. You are at peace again in the realization that all the appearances in the world are nothing and God is all.

And then, it is in that peace, and in the silence and stillness of that peace, that you *hear the still small voice*, or *hear the word of god*, or are *filled with the holy spirit*, or attain *realization*, or experience *enlightenment*, or receive *inspiration*. You simply be in peace and nothing else. The busy part of nothingizing the appearance is over now. Now you simply *be in peace*.

Don't look for what you think the *word of god or the still small voice* might be. Any concept you have of it will just disturb the peace only within which it can be revealed.

Joel's best description of it is: *The Thunder of Silence*. If you can't shake off all concepts altogether, then be in peace and listen for the thunder of silence. There is nothing explosive about realizing that God is all there is. And yet it is a thunderous realization: "All is well far beyond my wildest dreams, for God is always all there is." You just rest in the fact that God is all there is. There is no thought any more about the appearance you originally sat down to nothingize. Now you are simply being at peace in the realization that God is all.

I am awareness. I am not what fills my awareness, I am not the content of my awareness, I am awareness itself, the ability to be aware of anything.

Time Out

Meditations are "time outs" from the dream drama when we commune with God, when we remind ourselves of what we keep forgetting when we get back involved in the dream:

I am awareness. I am not what fills my awareness, I am not the content of my awareness, I am awareness itself, the ability to be aware of anything. I am not Ben, I am not a human, I am the awareness that is able to be aware of Ben, the awareness that is able to be aware of human identity. And now I leave behind all my concerns as a human being and I allow myself to dissolve into this pure awareness that I am. I just allow myself to slip into it like slipping into a crystal clear pool. I am not the human role I was playing in the fantasy dream of duality; I am this pure crystalline awareness, this utterly miraculous ability to know. This awareness is the very substance of God, and here it is the very substance of the I that I am. I am not human. I am not a personality. I am I. This I that I am is God. At first I see it only as a glimmer. I feel myself still holding on to my human sense of self and my personality, but gradually, gently, I start letting go of that grip, and as I do I feel myself melting into this I of me, this absolute center of my being, this substance of beingness itself, this unfathomable miracle of awareness. I do not resist my human sense of self, I do not judge it as good or bad; it is nothing and my response to it is nothing.

My spiritualized intellect has led me to this threshold by making it clear to me that the one thing that is true about me and God is that both God and I are awareness. God is all there is, this awareness that I am cannot be anything other than God. But that is only intellectual knowledge. It reports what is True and where that Truth is. Now I am looking where that Truth is. And where is that? It is at the absolute center of my being. It is the most essential part of me. It is that without which I would not know that I exist. It is my own awareness itself. And as I immerse myself into awareness and let go of my attachments to anything else, I find a peace, stillness, and an absolutely tranquil delight that has no parallel to anything I feel as a human being. It is as if I have entered another world, a world of infinite, pure, crystalline, fresh, clean, radiant, formless, dimensionless, empty space.

It's a world more real than my dream because it is a world consisting only of pure awareness, and awareness is the only thing that ever bestowed any reality to the dream in the first place. If I am not aware of the dream, it vanishes, because it never was anything in the first place. It was always only my awareness that was existing as nothing as the dream. This world, my awareness itself, my awareness itself being only aware of its own self as awareness, is the only world that is real. I am not between two worlds. The dream world does not exist. It is an illusion. It has no reality. I will return to it when I get up from this meditation, but I will be returning to a dream.

Now, I am forgetting about the dream for the moment and immersing myself into reality itself. This is only reality, my own unfathomably miraculous awareness. I have come before the throne of God, the holy of holies, and it is the one thing about me that I can be certain is true about myself -- that I am. I am on holy ground and must take off my shoes, my shoes of understanding. The One God of all reality absolute and infinite, is here, present, as the very core of my own being, the center of myself I refer to with the word "I".

Beliefs from the dream world keep echoing: "You're just one of billions of human beings who are born and die" -- beliefs that would murder Christ if they could. To them I say: "You lie. Get thee behind me Satan. Only by reason of my acceptance of you do you come to life. You have no life of your own. You have no existence of your own. You are nothing." And back my awareness turns from the distraction to itself, awareness, and I move into my own awareness just as if I were indeed approaching the Throne of God, because indeed that is what I am approaching.

And in silence, in absolute stillness, I feel what it feels like for my awareness to be the one and only absolute and infinite God. How much do I feel it? Just as much as I let go of my feelings of wanting to control the dream, of resisting the dream, of holding on to the dream. Just as much as I let go of my feelings of attraction or aversion to the dream. Just as much as I let go of the sense of self I carry around with me when I am in the dream. Just as much as I let go of my obsession with understanding reality. Just that much I melt into reality as I that I am and feel what it feels like to be the one and only absolute and infinite God. It electrifies me. It galvanizes me. It relaxes me. It enlivens me. It overwhelms me. It enraptures me.

How much further will I go this time? God is all there is and is completely located in me in the dimensionless center of my being as the very thing that I am -- awareness. How much further will I go? My awareness is God and God is being all there is. My awareness is being all there is. Lau-Tzu, Buddha, Jesus Christ, Joel Goldsmith, Lillian DeWaters, all live only in and as my awareness. All the infinite grandeur and splendor of the universe of galaxies, all of it exists only in and as my own infinite awareness. All the splendor and magnificence and wonder and beauty of the one and only absolutely infinite God exist only in and as this very awareness of mine that I am.

Again, I feel what it feels like for this to be true. Again, another layer of dream-feelings melt away. How much further shall I go this time? This is enough, this time. I am at peace. I am refreshed. I have communed with God. I open my eyes. And I get up to resume whatever it is given to me to do in the dream, until another hour or two when I feel the need for another "time out."

Nothing's holding you back. You are deliberately choosing to believe in duality.

Self Deception

The whole dream of duality is a self-deception, all of it and every last bit of it. It's nothing but self-deception. And to be thinking you are climbing out of the dream by trying to solve it like a murder mystery is merely more self-deception. To be thinking, "Oh, I'm working so hard towards attainment of the realization of God, with hours of meditation, more hours of study, practicing the presence and nothingizing and impersonalizing all day" is also merely more self deception.

If you think you're something other than God, you're simply deceiving yourself. It isn't anyone else that's deceiving you. It isn't a universal mass-consciousness belief in duality that's deceiving you. No. There isn't anything outside of you. Not even universal mass-consciousness belief in duality. There simply isn't anything else around that could be doing it to you. No. You are doing it to yourself. You are deceiving yourself.

Notice how we recoil a bit at the sound of all this. We immediately want to say, "NO, NO, NO, it's not all my fault!"

Well, no, it's not your fault. There is no fault. The self-deception was only a fantasy, an illusion, and it had no reality whatsoever. It was nothing but a dream and what went on in the dream never really happened. So there is nothing that ever went on that could be anyone's fault. God was always the only thing really going on, nothing else. That is why it's not your fault! You didn't do anything wrong. Your self-deception didn't create anything but a dream, it never harmed or jeopardized or destroyed or injured anything in any way, it was all a dream that never happened.

But so long as you do think it is happening, as long as you do think that the dream has some reality to it, then you might as well know that the entire dream is your own self-deception.

You are God. There is nothing else. The entire dream of something else is an illusion. God knows this. And you know this. So what is it that gets you to believe otherwise? Thinking there is something other than you? No. You know full well there isn't anything other than you. Well, then, there's nothing left but you! What is it that gets you to believe otherwise? You do!

Now why would you do that? You certainly make a big show of all this Infinite Way study and practice, all this hard work that's involved in realizing that you are God. But you are the only one who is getting you to believe you're anything other than God! It has to be you because there isn't anyone else around! And here you are doing all this spiritual discipline work to discover and correct whatever it is that is getting you to believe that you are something other than God. No. It's all a self deception to avoid the fact that it is simply you who are choosing to believe that God is not all there is.
After all, you do really know better. You already know that God is all there is. So it just wouldn't make any

sense for you, who already know God is all there is, to decide to believe that God is <u>not</u> all there is. And create a nightmare of distress, limitation and fear. So you deceive yourself into believing that it isn't really you but that it's something else other than you, a universal mass-consciousness belief in duality, and you're going to have to spend thousands of hours of meditation and nothingization before you can really get yourself free of this universal mass-consciousness belief in duality and once again experience yourself as you really are -- God.

It's all baloney. You're simply deceiving yourself. Why not admit it? Is it because you don't want to feel guilty? You're not guilty. You're not doing anything wrong. The dream doesn't affect God in any way whatsoever. And God is all there is. Stay in the dream as long as you want. It still isn't going to diminish God one bit. And God is all there is. So go ahead and stay in the dream if you want to. There's no rush. Take 20 years if you want to. There's nothing wrong with that. But don't deceive yourself into believing that if it were up to you, you would wake up instantly to the full realization of your divinity, but you can't because something's holding you back and it's going to take thousands of hours of meditation and practicing the *Infinite Way* before you're going to be able to overcome what's holding you back.

Nothing's holding you back. You are deliberately choosing to believe in duality. It's not happening to you. You are the only source. You are deliberately choosing to create the dream of duality you experience as your human life. The dream of duality appears as your life because you chose to believe in duality. Simply because you chose to believe that God is <u>not</u> all there is.

You don't have to figure out why you chose to believe this. It doesn't matter, because your choice to believe in duality did not create duality. The whole point of all this is that God remains absolutely and completely all there is no matter how much consciousness dreams of something other than God. Dreams about something other than God have always been, are now, and always will be nothing and therefore completely harmless.

Don't be so busy trying to change the dream. Just look at it differently. Realize that you ordered it up and that no matter what happens it can't hurt you or anyone else even the slightest bit. Look at it that way and let it be. Realize it's a dream about nothing and let it be. Realize that all the while, no matter what goes on in the dream, you are nothing but God being all there is.

Nobody else has to know. Only you need know. You don't have to change a thing. Leave it all alone. Let it all be. Just know you are God being all there is and the dream means nothing.

Another way to look at all this is to simply know that you are not the appearance you make in the dream. You are not in the dream for the purpose of awakening yourself. You are already awakened. You already know that God is all there is. You already know that you are God. You just keep getting deceived by the dream role you have. The dream role is simply not what you are. You are not the appearance you make in the dream. You're not the dream role. You are God. It doesn't matter how much your dream role still appears in the dream, it doesn't alter the fact that you are not the dream role. You are God.

You see, you already do know that you are God. It is the clearest thing, in fact, that you do know. God is all. There can't be anything else. Anything other than God simply isn't. It's not at all unclear. God is beingness itself. Nothing can be unless it's God. There is nothing other than beingness. Anything other than beingness is not being. It's couldn't be clearer. You're problem has nothing to do with increasing your understanding. You problem only has to do with your being deceived by the role you have in the dream.

You have been thinking that because you still have a physical body and still have to eat and sleep, and because you still have to do all sorts of things to take care of this body properly, and because your body is very limited in scope and ability, you have not yet attained full realization of what you really are. But that thought alone is what is giving you the feeling that you are enslaved to the role you happen to have in this dream. It's just your dream role. It's not you. You are God. The dream role is just a dream role. So stop resisting it. As soon as you begin releasing your resistance to the dream role you have, and soon as you stop wanting to change it, you will begin to feel less and less limited by it.

Sit and contemplate this in meditation, everything you know about yourself that identifies you as a particular human being is pure dream role, none of it is what you are. It doesn't matter in the least bit what the fabric of that dream role happens to be, whether that of a saint or a sinner, either way, the dream role is simply a dream role and isn't what you are.

God is not the greatest saint in the world. God is God

and any great saint is simply a role in the dream. There are no saints in heaven. God is God and any sinner is simply a role in the dream. There are no sinners in heaven.

Heaven is not a dream. There are no dream characters whatsoever in heaven. Nothing of the dream is in heaven. The entire dream is the fantasy of duality. The whole dream is about duality and nothing but duality. Heaven is pure oneness with not the slightest hint of duality.

Nothing of the dream is in heaven, except you. And nothing in heaven is in the dream, except you. You are heaven on earth. And you are the only thing on earth that is in heaven. Stop judging yourself by appearances. The appearances are only dream stuff that has no reality. You already know that very clearly. So stop judging yourself by appearances. Stop letting the appearance of the role you play within the dream deceive you in to thinking that that role is what you are. No. You couldn't come into the dream except that you assume a human identity, but the human identity is not what you are. You are not the appearance you make in the dream.

You are not a human being who is trying to discover his God-self. That too is just a role in the dream and it isn't what you are. Neither does it matter how devoted to God you are or how much you hate God; that too would just be a dream role in the dream.

The entire dream is an illusion. Stop trying to hammer at the dream to get it to behave more like God. Let the dream be what it is, the dream of duality. Stop trying to change the dream into heaven. Heaven already is. Making a parallel rendition of heaven within the dream of duality, no matter how sublime, could only be a dream about heaven and not heaven itself.

All that we call good within the dream is merely our dream about heaven, not heaven itself. And since it's a duality dream, our dream about heaven naturally requires that there be hell, too. The real Heaven, however, is not a dream. Heaven is reality. The dream is illusion. Don't try to change the dream. The dream is totally meaningless because the dream is the dream of duality and there is no duality. Nothing fantasized about duality can have any meaning whatsoever. Nothing that identifies you as a person within the dream has any meaning whatsoever. The only thing that has any meaning about you is that you are God. Isn't that enough? The dream role you play in the dream means absolutely nothing at all. So stop being deceived by the appearance of your dream role.

It doesn't matter one iota how much your dream role is appearing or what it is appearing as, it still is only a dream role and isn't what you are. So stop trying to change the dream role. The dream role is nothing. There is nothing there for you to change.

Trying to change it keeps engaging you into believing it is real. And the whole point of all this is for you to stop creating the illusion that anything other than God is real. *The more you keep trying to change the role you play in the dream, the more you engage yourself in believing the role is real, the more you engage yourself in believing that something other than God is real, and hence the more you create the dream of duality.* Contemplate this in your meditations. You are not the appearance you make in the dream. Notice all the things you think you are -- human, physical, limited, habitual, having desires and aversions, always trying to figure out and understand and so on. Don't try to change any of it. Let it all be. But just keep realizing: "I am not this. This is just my role in the dream. I am God."

After you do this for a while, you will feel like you are sitting in perfect peace in a location in space that coincides with your head. Don't stop there. Continue. You evidently believe you are consciousness occupying a particular area of space. You are not the appearance you make in the dream. You are God. God is all. There is nowhere where God is not. God is everywhere. Your experience of being in a particular location is not what you are. It is just part of the human identity role you are playing in the dream. Don't resist it. Don't try to change it. Don't try to imagine what it would be like if your human identity experience of limited consciousness were to expand out to fill all space. That's trying to re-engineer the dream to fit heaven's blueprint. Your business is not to create a rendition of heaven in the dream, but to wake up to the real heaven that already exists.

Quit trying to use your knowledge of Truth to fix the dream. Simply use your knowledge of truth to wake up from the dream. Use your knowledge of Truth to realize that you are not anything connected with the role you play in the dream. Use your knowledge of Truth to realize that you are God no matter what your role identity in the dream happens to be.

The belief in something other than God is very powerful and pervasive.

The Most Dangerous
Idea in the World

"What you are saying is dangerous. You must explain it more carefully, because otherwise some may use it to justify an indulgence in license, and do all manner of things that may be hurtful to themselves, or to others, or to society; or even worse, some may use it to justify a desire to flee from the world rather than engage in it."

Please understand that my reply to this will appear harsh only because it will confront you with fears that, although they are fears about nothing, remain barriers to your spiritual emergence as long as they remain hidden. It's a very, very delicate operation to coax someone to confront their fears. But you ask a question that cannot be answered any other way. Just keep in mind as you read that my purpose is not to frighten you, but to enable you to nothingize fears that are creating the appearance of confinement in your life.

Fleeing from the world can never work, because the world is exactly as you created it to be. You will only create another world that appears just as perilous and painful as the one you fled. Why? *Because you are terrified of the idea of relating to the world always as if it were never, never, never anything but God.*

To open yourself up to absolutely everything you experience of the world as you would open up to God Himself. Admit it. The idea is more than a little terrifying. There is always that threshold of terror, that wall of fire, which all major mystics allude to.

This is the real reason why the full impact of God being all there is hasn't dawned on you completely yet. This is why you hold yourself back from realizing its full impact. Not because you can't. But because you are terrified of what that would really be like.
It's even possible that you have been avoiding even thinking about what that would really be like. What would it be like to be loving and trusting everything you encountered in your world as if it were God himself in his entirety? It's just way, way, way too much. So you have to take it slow.

There's nothing wrong with taking it slow, but if you want to speed it up then you will have to look at what it is that you are afraid of. You are afraid that there is danger in the world. You are afraid that there is sin (or license), and the possibility of injury or harm to be both inflicted and received. You are afraid that you might be in jeopardy of both inflicting injury and being victim to it, either of which would be a very ugly place to be.

The belief in something other than God is very powerful and pervasive. Why, you just can't walk out the door and walk around loving God all day long. Even if you could pull it off, they would lock you up or make you a saint. It's too extreme. It's not practical. And practical means making proper provisions for possibilities of evil; like food, clothing, shelter, money, insurance policies, investments and technology. Why, if anyone were to simply turn around and ignore all of that, they would put him in a mental institution. It's all far, far too extreme.

So you settle in to your safe and familiar cocoon and make a game out of the extent to which you can conjure up a miraculous healing here and there, like fireworks in the night, as long as it stays fairly dark, so that you don't have to see what we are so terrified of.

It's like the old trust game when you would close your eyes and fall back and trust your friends to catch you. This whole God realization thing is very much like that. You would have to put our entire life into freefall and trust nothing at all but God, if you were to walk out the door and relate to absolutely every aspect of that world as you would relate to God Himself. And even if you threw yourself into God's arms in total surrender, in a radiant ecstasy of trust, the fruits would be so extraordinary that you would live as *the word made flesh* or *Emmanuel* (God with us). It's too much.

But what is it about all those luminous major mystics anyway? Isn't it simply a matter of the fact that evil disappears wherever they go? And why would evil disappear wherever they go? It is quite simple really. They simply know that evil does not exist! Only god exists!!! Yes, sometimes we almost have to shout it to ourselves when we find that here we have all over again created another reality of duality.

For all of us duality dreamers, the most dangerous idea in the world is the idea that there is no such thing as danger. The idea that there is no such thing as danger, is only dangerous, however, to the mind that still believes in duality. If that mind de-conditions itself from believing in duality, it will then be the transparency for the knowledge that only God is, only God, only God; no evil, not even the teeniest, tiniest bit of evil, none, not now, not ever.

There is no danger and there never, ever has been or will be any danger anywhere. That's the truth. That's the way it is. Everything else is pure, unadulterated, absolute *fantasy* with absolutely no reality to it in any fashion whatsoever. *That's* what those major mystics know. But they don't just know it. They've thrown their entire selves into it in a total freefall. And consequently wherever they go, evil disappears and all of us dreamers are amazed at the miracles and healings that appear to be connected to them.

You know, it wouldn't be very much fun to play that trust game when you were a kid, if every time you closed your eyes and were to fall back into the arms that you're supposed to completely trust your friends to provide, you instead swung around as you fell, "just in case" those friends of yours don't come through. We keep fantasizing about the freefall, and even fancy ourselves doing it here and there. But we always swing around before we would hit that floor just in case God doesn't come through. We only rarely set it up so that we depend on God and God alone. We still pretty well take care of ourselves. And since that's the practical and responsible thing to do, we can feel practical and responsible instead of feeling afraid.

The Truth, however, is that there is nothing to be afraid of, there never was, nor will there ever be. There's only God. It's not an easy pill to swallow! But that's only because it's so hard for us to accept that there really is nothing to be afraid of. The more we think about what we would do if we really did believe it was that way, the more we frighten ourselves: Someone could feel perfectly justified jumping off a building, or even blowing up the building, because nothing he ever does could ever alter the fact that God is always all there is.

We don't trust the world to be totally God to that extent. We are not willing to go into that much freefall. But what if the person doesn't really know God, and in throwing caution to the wind ends up becoming one of the destitute homeless people. It gets even more frightening when it dawns on us that Jesus, too, was a destitute homeless person.

We can't cushion the ride from fear all the way through. Ask Babaji to be your teacher and he will ask you to jump off the Himalayan cliff.. Then, after your fellow disciples collect your broken body and Babaji miraculously heals it, you'll be ready for the lessons that lie ahead. The fears have to be confronted to be nothingized. Running from our fears and deceiving ourselves with some intellectual nothingization exercises, naturally will not work.

But we can't push anyone into confronting their fears. People don't like to be pushed off cliffs. They can be advanced *Infinite Way* students too and they still don't like to be pushed off cliffs. And yet, if they trusted God completely they wouldn't have any problem with it at all. It's very, very clear that we do not trust God that much. That's the only reason we don't like to be pushed off cliffs. We're afraid of danger. We're afraid of something other than God.

You might think, "But really now, you keep on like this, and no one is going to listen to you, and worse than that people will shun you as a madman." You see that is just more evidence of how frightened people really are. People are simply afraid of the truth. And there is no way to realize the truth without confronting those fears and nothingizing them.

You already know there is no danger, no evil, nothing but God. You're practically blue in the face for knowing it so hard. Now you have to welcome all those hidden feelings into that knowing. Don't run from what you fear in order to avoid the feeling of fear. Be courageous. Admit the fear. Acknowledge it. Let go of all of your resistance to it. Feel it without labeling it good or bad. And then nothingize it.

There may be those who will feel obliged to say: "These are deranged, unsafe, dangerous, unsound, maniacal, anarchist, and radical ideas that can only lead to tragedy."

There will also be those who will no longer run from the fear, who will more and more go into freefall, who will begin to trust the world more and more to be what it always has been and always will be -- God.

God is absolute Authority. The only way I could create the illusion of being something other than God was to abrogate my authority as God.

Be Still, and Know that I am God"

A very dear friend called today with a most interesting experience. He had just returned from a trip to the dentist and had replaced the use of Novocain with the use of the phrase, "Be Still and Know that I am God." He explained to me how he would address all the discomforts caused by the dental drills with that simple phrase, and how those discomforts appeared to obey the command.

His only problem was the discomfort of the dentist himself, who was uneasy about drilling a patient's teeth without numbing the area first. After two teeth were drilled and filled without Novocain, the dentist said to my friend, "Now, believe me, this third tooth is definitely not going to be any fun to drill without anesthetic." And sure enough, the discomfort of drilling the third tooth did not obey the command to "Be Still," and Novocain had to be injected. The phrase had authority over two teeth, but not over the third. The belief of the dentist retained authority over the third.

Everything we've explored in these writings up to this point all boils down to saying, "Be Still, and Know that I am God." I am God. I want to wake up from the dream that I am not God. So to anything that appears as part of this dream of not being God I say, very simply, "Be Still, and Know and I am God." There is nothing else to do. There is nothing else worth doing. It is the answer to every situation I meet in life, and the only answer that makes any sense.

Lack of supply? "Be Still, and Know that I am God, all supply is what I am and all there is." Self doubts? Worries? Fears? Guilts? Pain? Compulsions? Addictions? Confusion? Illness? Stress? Pressure? Confinement? Heartbreak? Sorrow? Frustration? It matters not what the experience is. The only answer to any of it is "Be Still, and Know that I am God." There is nothing else to say, nothing else to think, nothing else to do, just that and that alone.

And so I meet each experience of life with absolute authority, "Be Still, and Know that I am God." Either the experience is the experience of myself, as God, being all there is, or, the experience is a non-existent fantasy about my not being God, in which case the only answer that makes any sense is "Be Still, you dream that I am not God, Be Still now, and Know that I am God."

Here is where spiritualized intellect ceases as such and vectors upwards as Authority. God is absolute Authority. The only way I could create the illusion of being something other than God was to abrogate my authority as God. But when I say, "Be Still, and Know that I am God," I am reclaiming my Godly Authority. There is nothing in the world that appears to be other than God that I do not have absolute authority over, and to which I cannot say, with the authority of God,

"Be Still, and Know that I am God, there is nothing but me, and all that appears to be other than me is nothing, never was, and never will be, so be still, you apparitions of nothing, and know that I am God. You are not God, you that pose as the possibility of something other than God. By your very nature, you are not God, because you present yourself only as something other than God. But I am all and you are nothing, so Be Still, and know that I am God. Be still, you are not at all what you appear to be, you can only be the God that I am, all there can be, infinite harmony. Be still, you who perceive something other than God, and know that I am God and there is no other, I am all, I am the entirety of all there is, I am the totality of all there is, I am the completeness, perfection, absoluteness and infinity of all there is."

Oh, yes indeed, the meaning of those words will expand and deepen unfathomably, but there is no need to keep a diary of it, there is only the need to do it. i already know it. Now I must do it. I must deflect my momentum from the vector of spiritualized intellect to the magnitude of authority. Either I shall appreciate an experience as God in absolute fullness or I shall tell whatever it is that seems less than God to "Be Still, knock it off, we're not falling for it anymore, I am God and all there is, is God."

I must stop wasting so much time walking around in the stupor of duality. I shall no longer pat myself on the back for doing 15 meditations, and 22 nothingizations in a day, for heavens sake. What was I doing all the rest of the time? I was allowing myself to float back into the stupor of duality, wherein I do all kinds of things motivated by the duality paradigm. That's stupid. That's Moses leading me around in circles in the desert. Every single last experience that comes my way during the day, either I shall appreciate it as God in absolute fullness or tell whatever it is that seems less than God to "Be Still, and Know that I am God." I shall not do anything else! What else is there to do? Go along with the appearance of something less than God because I'm taking a break from living the *Infinite Way*?

Each and every experience that comes my way, Can I appreciate it as God in full manifestation? If not, well then why not? And whatever comes up as answer to the question "why not?" is that to which I shall say, "Be Still and know that I am God." If I don't do that, then I am going along with the appearance of something other than God, and I am surrendering my authority as God to this *something* that appears to be something other than God. That's a very, very debilitating thing to do. But it's the only other thing I can be doing if i am not responding to the appearance with "Be Still and Know that I am God" until such time as I experience what the appearance was a distortion of: God in full manifestation.

To what, or to whom, are you saying "Be Still?" You say this only and always, to yourself. Remember, there is no one else. There is only one person in the world, you and everybody else who is you, too. But why are you saying, "Be Still?" To quite down something you didn't stir up? Of course not! If it needs to be stilled, you must have stirred it up. Nothing or anyone else could, because there is nothing else. And what is it that you have stirred up? You stirred the dream of duality, of course. The world being divided up into opposites, good and evil, beautiful and ugly, pleasure and pain, health and illness, success and failure, love and hate, peace and war, wealth and poverty, happiness and sadness, easy and hard, inside and outside, you and everything else. Evil is not a lie about good, rather the opposites of good and evil are a lie about God.

And what is God if God is neither good nor evil? Absolute! The absolute is the only thing that has no opposite. The absolute is the only thing that is not dual or polar. Only the absolute is. Goodness, beauty, happiness, success and love do not exist. They are just as much part of the dream of duality as is evil, ugliness, sadness, failure and hatred. Only the absolute is. Because only the absolute is absolutely all there is and all there can be. There is nothing that can be its opposite because it is absolutely all there is besides which there cannot be anything else. The opposite of being is not non-being, because non-being isn't and therefore cannot be an opposite. Neither can you be something other than the absolute because the absolute is absolutely all there can be.

Hence I am absolute, I am the one besides which there is no other. I am God. be still, dream of duality, dream of something other than the absolute, be still, and know that I am absolute, know that I am all there is, know that I being one is all there is, know that wholeness, completeness, perfection, infinity is all there is.

Nothing isn't the polar opposite of all there is, as poverty is the polar opposite of wealth in the dream.

Nothing hasn't a reality as the whole dream of duality has no reality. Fragmentation is not the polar opposite of wholeness, as disintegration is the polar opposite of integration in the dream, because fragmentation is impossible for the absolute, as the whole dream itself is absolutely impossible. Incompleteness is not the polar opposite of completeness because completeness is all there is making it impossible for incompleteness to be, just as it is impossible for the dream of duality to be. Imperfection is not the polar opposite to perfection, as relative degrees of precision are opposite to relative degrees of imprecision in the dream, because perfection is all there can be, besides which imperfection is impossible. Limitation is not the polar opposite to infinity, as lack is the polar opposite to abundance in the dream, because infinity is all there is and therefore limitation isn't.

Duality is impossible for God because God is all there is. We cannot turn around and say that since God is all there is, duality too must be God, because duality is the proposition that God is not all there is. One is all there is, not two. From the dreamers' viewpoint it may look like greater health and less disease, but to you it is simply the wholeness and perfection of the absolute. From the dreamers' viewpoint it may look like greater wealth and less poverty, but to you it is simply the infinity of the absolute. And some dreamers may applaud you for doing well in the duality game, but you are not playing the duality game. You simply know that one is all. You are not trying to accumulate good and avoid evil, or accumulate wealth and avoid poverty, or develop good health and avoid disease. All you are doing is "being still and knowing that I am one.

Ontological Mysticism   Ben Gilberti

Seeking pleasure is every bit as illusory as avoiding pain. Both are movements in alignment with duality and contrary to the principle of oneness. The pleasure/pain experience of life arises from the notion that all is not one, and since all is one, the pleasure/pain experience of life is an illusion.

But this does not mean that the illusion is bad. If we make that assessment we are still dancing to the duality tune. The illusion is not to be avoided as we avoid pain in the pleasure/pain experience of life. The illusion is not something unfortunate or tragic in the way in which we polarize life in duality. The illusion is just the readout of the duality software, the transformations projected from a hologram imbedded with the (mis) information of duality.

The illusion is nothing more than what duality looks like, merely the appearance of something that doesn't exist. As Joel Goldsmith would say, "The hypnotism has no power." You might still see it, but if what you are seeing is what duality looks like, you are seeing something that has no substance, reality or power. If you are trying to acquire it or avoid it, you are still operating under the hypnotic spell of duality. The illusion is nothing to be avoided, nor anything to be sought, because it is nothing.

The pleasure/pain experience of life is an illusion because there is nothing to avoid that would qualify as pain, and there is nothing to seek that would qualify as pleasure; rather everything simply is, absolutely, totally, completely, entirely, perfectly, harmoniously and infinitely.

That which is, *is not better than* illusion. If you see the Truth as being a great deal better than the illusions of duality you are simply making the same old mistake of judging this good and that bad that has been keeping you locked up inside your dualistic paradigm in the first place. The illusion is not bad or evil in any way whatsoever. All there is, is the absolute infinite perfection of one consciousness being all there is. It is not good because there is nothing else besides it which could qualify as bad.

Only so long as the proposition is believed that something other than that which is can exist can a dual judgment perspective exist. There in we see everything as falling on the spectrum between good and evil creates the appearance of reality consisting of good and evil.

When you, after learning that there is only one, not two, say that the one that is, is good, and much to be desired over the illusion of that which isn't, you have set yourself into the *seek this, avoid that* momentum that creates the illusory appearance of duality in the first place. The illusion of duality isn't bad in the slightest degree the illusion of duality is simply an illusion of duality, a fantasy about nothing. It's not bad, it just isn't.

When you know that an appearance of duality simply does not exist, and you also have let go of the habit of seeking good and avoiding bad, you will rest in perfect calm and absolute tranquility right smack in the middle of the appearance without the slightest inclination to avoid it as bad while at the same time knowing with absolute certainty that the appearance is an insubstantial apparition of nothing.

Ontological Mysticism   Ben Gilberti

You don't try to make yourself see it as nothing because you're trying to avoid it as bad. That will lock you up. It's not bad. Nothing is bad or good. Rather, the one beingness is.

So do not try to avoid or escape duality. Be still in the midst of anything. There is nothing to avoid. There is nothing to acquire or reach or find or attain. Judge nothing good or bad and all will simply be what it is -- God.

> *They said to Him: Shall we then, being children, enter the Kingdom? Jesus said to them: When you make the two one, and when you make the inner as the outer and the outer as the inner and the above as the below, and when you make the male and the female into a single one, then you shall enter the Kingdom.*
> (The Gospel of St. Thomas)

You must change the dual mode of perception. The twofold mode of perception is to perceive reality as broken up into two, you and all that is not you.

Nothingizing the Dual Mode of Perception

There is no separate self set apart from the world. There is no separate knower set apart from what is known. There is no separate awareness set apart from what awareness is aware of. There is no you set apart from the world. The world is you and you are the world.

Your first concern cannot be what you are to do in the world, but rather how you perceive it. There will no doubt be a change in action, but only because first occurred a change in perception.

The basic duality is between the illusion you call self outside of which, consequently, is the illusion called non-self or your world. Your world is you and your world. It is you and everything that is not you. That is the basic duality. It's not just a belief stored in your mind on the basis of which you act. It's not just that. Of far, far more impact than that is that it is, in addition to being a belief, a way of perceiving, a way of looking at things, a way of feeling your relationship to things. Just changing the belief in duality will do very little. You must change the dual mode of perception. The twofold mode of perception is to perceive reality as broken up into two, you and all that is not you. There is no you that is separate and apart from the world.

When you sit in meditation and contemplate *I* and in effect look for the real you, the pure *I* that is God what do you find? Is there a pure *I* sitting in a chair with a whole world going on outside the house? If you find such a thing, who is it that is aware of this pure *I* sitting in a chair with a whole world outside? Who? Are you as pure awareness? Ok. And who is aware of that? Pure awareness again, you say? Pure awareness aware of pure awareness, you say? Ok. And who is aware of that?

You cannot any longer find a self to separate as the separate observer of something other than itself.

It's an unnerving experience because we cling for dear life to this Satan self we have that is separate from all it experiences, and yet now we cannot find this self, now the act of dual perception is impossible. Pure awareness is always being aware only of itself. Ask who is aware of this as an observer and there isn't any other than itself, pure awareness; there's nothing dual, there is no longer the observer and the observed, the observer and the observed are one.

Now, you don't climb down from this summit of enlightenment and re-enter a real world wherein you are separate from what you perceive. If you do, it is only because you decide to continue the act of dual perception, saying to yourself, I am is the observer. This that I observe is other than what I am. With that act of perception you create the dream of duality and all its problems and conflicts and fears.

Think for a moment of the universe you are aware of. Start with your city, then the whole of humanity, then all life, then the entire planet, then the galaxy, then the universe of galaxies. Now, for a moment, stop creating the perception all of this exists separately from the awareness that is aware of it. See it all as awareness itself. See it all as you. If you still feel like there is a you apart from it all, go look for that you again, and again when you cannot find it, you will again be left with the only *you that remains* -- the entire universe you are aware of. You and the universe and awareness are all one. Don't just know it, see it that way.

There are no boundaries outside of which is to be found the other. I am all. This entire universe is nothing but the sound of my being; the resonance, the reverberation, the music, the symphony of my own being, a symphony of light and sound and rhythms of infinite variety. All of it is my own self being, all of it is the music of my own self being.

The universe is not a dream. The dream is the stupor wherein you believe and behave and experience as though the universe were not your own self being. When you awaken from the dream, the Universe and all that it is up to does not change. What changes is your perception of it. Whereas before you perceived it all to be something other than you and outside of you, now you realize that the entirety of it is you and you alone and no one else but you. This entire universe, every last atom and electron, every galaxy, every love, and every dream, all of it without exception, is the sound, the music, the symphony of your being. That's not the dream. That's you being the entire universe. The dream is that you're not the entire universe but an infinitesimal part of it. The dream is that you are not as intimately one with everything as possible -- one with everything because everything is you.

When you wake up, the universe stays. When you wake up the universe doesn't turn out to all have been a dream. The universe is <u>not</u> the dream. The dream is only that you are not the universe. That's all. Everything else about the dream, or stupor, or hypnotic trance, or mesmerism, or fantasy, or illusion or appearance, is all derivative of the idea that you are not the universe.

Contemplate that. You are the universe. You can still go on naming and categorizing and counting and measuring and formulating formulas to reflect that nature of the universe. But the ultimate formula about the nature of the universe is $I=uc^2$. I Equals the Universe times the speed of light squared. Contemplate that. *I Equals the Universe times the speed of light squared.* Right now you perceive the universe as mass, inertia, matter, physical, and external. In your mind, convert all that mass into energy. It is only your mind and your mind's belief in duality, your mind's belief in "something other," that makes the energy of the universe appear to be tied up with itself in what appears as mass. But when the tied up energy of mass is untied it releases all that tied up energy in an energy release that is equivalent to 35,000,000 (c^2) times the inertia represented by the mass. That's what it feels like within the dream as the dreamer wakes up to the fact that all the so-called mass in the universe is nothing but the music of his consciousness being. In that moment $I=uc^2$. In that moment you will have nothingized the dual mode of perception.

Ontological Mysticism   Ben Gilberti

It's your universe. You were the only one
who thought it up. When you know that,
you are no longer bound by it.

Ontological Mysticism   Ben Gilberti

The Space Between Thoughts

My friend called me again last night, (the same one who prefers stillness over Novocain), and told me Deepak Chopra was on PBS. Like any teacher, Deepak has his own style and attracts those who will benefit most from it, mostly those in love with scientific paradigms. But Deepak (I like to call him Deeptalk) is also a virtuoso artist. He has as good a handle on the nature of reality as any mystic, but the artistry with which he communicates it surpasses Fulton Sheen's (who was a Bishop, rather than a mystic). As always, Deeptalk left me in tears, much in the same way Rubenstein or Van Cliburn can do the same.

"Slip into the space between thoughts," says Deepak. And what is it that you find in between thoughts? Yes, it is the thinker, all right, but not the thinker you thought you were. It is the thinker that has thought up the entire universe.

It's your universe. You were the only one who thought it up. When you know that, you are no longer bound by it. When you know it is only what you have thought up, possibilities become infinite, whereas when you thought it was something created by some other source, possibilities were extremely narrow. Your center of reference is no longer the role you are playing in the dream, but rather your awareness of yourself as the one awareness that is creating the entire universe. Your center of reference is no longer as a part of the holographic projection of the universe, but the hologram itself in which *all of it is in each bit of it*. That now is much more real to you than your human role. You have <u>no</u> more fear, you need <u>no</u> more approval, you <u>no</u> more desire to control, and you can <u>no</u> longer be offended.

All of this has a rather profound effect on how you act out your local human role, but that's only because reality is now known to be universal rather than local. All of that has a profound outcome on the bit part you play in the dream, but that's only because you know that all of it is in each bit of it. The human role is only one tiny bit of what you've thought up so far. The entire evolution of life on this planet for the past 4 billion years has been nothing less and nothing other than you thinking up the world you now find yourself in. Beyond this there are billions of planets elsewhere in this same universe thinking up worlds to experience. All of it nothing but the one you, which is all there is thinking up an infinity of worlds to experience.

Deepak was at his peak of profundity, however, when he declared, "If you cannot see God in a rainbow or a flower, you will never find Him anywhere else." To know that your body is this amazing transformation of information all thought up by your consciousness is a very sensuous experience. "Be consciousness in each atom of your body," says Deepak.

The taboo against sensuousness originates from the intention to keep people locked into the dream. If a person's center of reference is the human role instead of the universal identity, he manipulates others to keep them doing the things that support his human role. If that human role itself becomes very powerful, (like a Bishop for example), and if that power was considered to be real, then the manipulation of many, many people is necessary. The taboo against sensuousness, the indictment and conviction of Eros as evil, effectively puts us at odds with the entirety of our creation as the universe, since we know this creation only through our senses.

You are the one who has been thinking all of this all up. You thought up your body. You can review the whole process of thinking it up by reviewing the evolution of life on this planet. If you can be seduced to think that what you have thought up is half good and half evil, and especially if you can be seduced to think that the senses of the body are evil, then you will be alienated from yourself. Thereby castrated and made impotent. When this happens you need the services of those who seduced you, whose position of power is now more firmly secured. This is because you have accepted the idea that incapacitates you, the idea that sensuousness is evil. It doesn't matter on what side of the master/slave coin you happen to be on this time around, whether you're subjugator or subjugated, it's all the same two-bit part, and both sides get thoroughly jammed.

Experience your life to the fullest extent, experience all you have created to the fullest extent, judging none of it as good nor evil. You thought it all up for the purpose of experiencing it. Don't buy into the nonsense that's designed to get you jammed. Don't buy into the nonsense that some of it is good and some of it is bad, and that you would be bad if you allowed yourself to experience some of it. It's just a trick to debilitate you by estranging you from your infinite self.

The entire universe is this infinite self, all of it, your body, and all evolutionary life everywhere. You thought this universe up as a paradise, to be experienced in bliss. Not the happiness or pleasure you nibble on like crumbs from the ultimate master's table, not the happiness always in peril of becoming sadness, or the pleasure always in peril of becoming pain, but the bliss of one infinite being knowing and being it's infinite potentiality in infinite expression. It's all right there. But you have to be open to sensuous experience to experience it because it is a sensuous experience itself.

Sit in meditation as Deepak suggests and slip in-between the thoughts, be consciousness as each atom of your body and you will indeed feel your body as a bubbling swirl of consciousness. It will be a sensuous experience.

Each meditation should be a dip into the pool of ecstasy, but only if you can allow yourself to feel. So let go of all your judgments about your feelings. That which you can totally allow yourself to feel, is that which you can let go of effortlessly.

This becomes the great paradox of the Infinite Way, only when there is no longer any resistance to a creation whatsoever can that creation be allowed to dissolve. It's true it's all illusion, yes, but that is to say it is absolutely malleable -- it can be something else, as Lillian DeWaters liked to do with it on occasion, or it can be nothing, as mystical healers do for a living -- either way, to realize it is an illusion means that it is absolutely malleable -- it doesn't have to be what it appears to be now -- it can be anything, or it can be nothing -- there is infinite potentiality, infinite possibility. That's what it means to realize it is an illusion.

Realize that you and nobody but you thought the illusion up, and if you remain alienated to it by buying into that nonsense that some of it is good and some of it is bad, you're going to stay stuck with the notion that you are a limited being in mortal peril. Don't buy it. Experience yourself with no alienation at all, no reservations, no resistances, no judgments, totally accepting it all as your own creation.

My own will cannot be anything other than
God's will because God is all there is.

                    Ben Gilberti

God's Will and Lucifer's

I might do something dangerous, I might do something evil, I might become Lucifer, the great deceiver, rebellious of God's absolute sovereignty, and saying as they do in witches covens: Do what thou wilt, there is no God to obey.

Am I doing God's will, or not? If I am not doing God's will, then I am asserting my own will over and above that of God's will, and have become Lucifer, he who asserts his own will over God's.

To say that God is all there is, is to say that there is only one will, that of God's. The role I play, the actions that I take, the things that I do, either they are expressing God's will or they are expressing some other will. There is no other will besides God's. If I believe there is I will create an illusory appearance of it in the form of my own will as opposed to God's.

My own will cannot be anything other than God's will because God is all there is. But if I believe my own will can be something other than God's I will create the illusion of my own will appearing to be contrary to God's will.

But that only happens to the extent that I consider

physical survival, or the well-being of my local self, important. Everything I do for no other reason but to insure the well-being of my physical self is done from the illusory appearance of a will other than God's will. Everything I do for no other reason but that it pleases my physical senses is done from the illusory appearance of a will other than God's will. Everything I do that is solely for the benefit of my local self is done from the illusory appearance of a will other than God's will.

Everything that I do for the benefit of all consciousness everywhere is done from a will that is in fact all will could ever be -- God's will. Take no thought as to what I shall eat, or how I will be clothed. Rather listen for God's inspiration as to how I can be of benefit to all consciousness everywhere, and make that the will from which I do anything that I do. If I hope to become a star by being of benefit to all consciousness everywhere, that intention comes from the illusory appearance of a will other than God's will.

Lucifer does indeed get annihilated in all the archetype stories about him, because Lucifer doesn't exist. If I intend anything other than God's will or that which is of benefit to all consciousness everywhere then I have created myself to be Lucifer in peril of inevitable annihilation. The whole thing is a dream about something that never was or could be. Although I'll give myself one hell of a nightmare while I believe it could be. God doesn't intend to be in a nightmare. That isn't God's will. And the will I think I have that creates the nightmare that I think I'm in, doesn't exist any more than the nightmare it creates. Indeed, the nightmare doesn't matter because it isn't real, but to deliberately intend that which creates or supports the illusion of the nightmare is Satanic.

Satanic will doesn't matter because it isn't possible. To deliberately intend that which creates or supports the illusion of Satanic will inject my consciousness into the satanic identity, and there I stay imprisoned. Incarcerate in fear and jeopardy, caught in a dream that isn't real, all because I believed it was possible for me to have a will other than God's. All of it to vanish with no remembrance once I accept that God is all there is. Ultimately couldn't matter because God is always all there is. I only realize and experience this only if I have not deceived myself into believing that something other than God is possible. Anytime I intend to do anything that even slightly suggests that God is not all there is, I am creating or supporting the illusion experienced as the nightmare. I am in the illusion of what it would be like if God weren't all there is.

I could decide to be Lucifer wholeheartedly and when I woke up it wouldn't matter at all. Every time I decide to be Lucifer, suddenly the whole world is made of Lucifers. All of them doing their own thing instead of God's will, and I'm in the Devil's Kingdom -- Hell. Make no mistake about it the dream of duality is hell. It's totally unreal, alright, but every time I decide to be Lucifer, every time I imagine myself to be someone who can do something that is not of benefit to the whole of consciousness everywhere, I am creating and sustaining the illusion of duality. I am creating and sustaining my own nightmare of hell that I make such a fuss about wanting to get out of.

There is such a thing as God's will. It's the only will there can be. What is God's will? What does God intend? Does God intend he be broken into parts, and one part of him benefit at the expense of another part? Certainly not, he would intend to be of benefit to his whole self, all consciousness everywhere. How are we to be of benefit to all consciousness everywhere? By being totally open to divine Inspiration. As I commune with God in meditations, remembering and experiencing your oneness with God, I will know what God's will is as the union of inspiration and love, I will know it to be the only will there is, God's will, your own will, the will that is the inspiration to love. I will be in freefall because I will take no thought about how I should survive. My only thought will be how I shall love. I will have moved myself out of the way, I will have let go of all the concerns about the well-being and survival of your local self out of the way. In this way I can be a transparency for the expression of God's will -- Love.

This consciousness that I am is actually the substance of which this universe is made, and the substance of which my body is made.

Ontological Mysticism   Ben Gilberti

God's Will and Yours

What is all this lugubrious hand-wringing about devilish possibilities of action contrary to God's will? It seems the belief in duality, if we let it, will lay out its red carpet for us every inch along the spiritual path, making it always strewn with new and more monumental dangers the further along the path we travel.

What is this will of God that I agonize over being in alignment with or not? Is God orchestrating the Great Awakening, like a commander in chief, through ranks of Ascended Masters in the heavens and Enlightened Ones on earth who receive their orders from God by reason of their advanced ability to listen to the "Still Small Voice," and who carry out their orders as part of a Cosmic Team that dances to God's tune?

Is that what's going on? Did Jesus, Lau Tzu, Buddha, Joel Goldsmith, and Lillian DeWaters all do what they did in their lives as part of a grand choreography? Was this only comprehensible to the infinite intelligence that planned it? When Jesus decided to walk from Galilee to Capernaum, does he do so because he got a message from the Father to do so? Or is it rather that Jesus' consciousness was such that his own determination to take the walk is automatically one with the Father's will by reason of his awareness of his oneness with the Father?

There is no separation between your will and God's will. Any idea that there can be a separation, is illusion grown out of the belief in duality, as well as is all the hand-wringing about the perils of a will separate from God's. It was all nothing more than the belief in duality trying to catch up with your spiritual progress and sink its claws into it.

This consciousness that I am is actually the substance of which this universe is made, and the substance of which my body is made. Everything is made out of consciousness. Everything is made out of the consciousness that I am made of. It is this consciousness out of which the whole universe is made that I really am. This person called Ben Gilberti with whom I've been identifying is only one swirl of information in this consciousness within which swirls the entire universe.

This very consciousness that I am at this very moment is swirling up within itself the magnificent symphony of light, sound, and feeling we call the universe. This very consciousness that I am is David Bohm's implicate order. And it is Deepak Chopra's quantum mechanical holographic potential of infinite possibility, from which my informational beliefs project, like a hologram, the entire world.

The beliefs that are in alignment and harmony with the principle of oneness are the intelligible beliefs of the one infinite intelligence knowing infinite oneness. The beliefs that are not in alignment and harmony with the principles of oneness are the unintelligible beliefs. These beliefs give me the impression that I exist only as the limited human role or personality with which I have identified.

Ontological Mysticism   Ben Gilberti

Even when I remain asleep and think that I am no more than a personality, it is still my own beliefs. It is my own creation of information, which results in every last bit of the transformation, I see as an infinite external macrocosm and microcosm.

Even when I remain asleep, it is still my own very consciousness that is the sole and only source of it all. I nothingize the beliefs that are not in alignment with the principle of oneness. As I take those beliefs and discern the truth that each of them was about, the more I perceive the principle of oneness rather than believe the beliefs of multiplicity. The dance of multiplicity becomes a symphony of oneness and harmony rather than a cacophony of duality.

We know that what we are is the one infinite consciousness with infinite potentiality. Hence we know that all the information that this infinite consciousness creates is an expression of its own consciousness of infinite oneness or harmony. All its information is infinite intelligence knowing the infinite intelligibility of infinite oneness. Anything less or other than that is the knowledge of something that is not intelligible.

All consciousness is consciousness. The idea of there being something other than consciousness is incomprehensible. Anything other than consciousness is only by reason of its being known by consciousness.

Even if we pretend that duality exists, even if we pretend that something other than consciousness exists, it still is only the one consciousness that pretends such a thing. Even while consciousness dreams its illusion of duality, all the while, it is only the one consciousness that has such a dream. Even while we dream of disharmony, that dream of disharmony is dreamt by a reality whose total oneness remains absolutely intact. When you know a dream's a dream, the dream offers no threat.

As the information that consists of this dream of otherness that cannot be is seen to be a dream of what isn't, the reality of the oneness of the dreamer that is becomes the frame of reference in which we live and move and have our being, and that which we dreamt of being that has no being is no longer imagined to be.

The consciousness that I am is God being all there is. What is it that is blocking my experience of that? The fact that it just isn't anything like the personality I'm pretending to be. It's not even close. The personality I'm pretending to be is anything but "God being all there is." Quite the contrary, the personality I'm pretending to be knows very little, has very limited intelligence, needs all kinds of things like food and shelter and clothing and comfort and sleep. This pretend persona has all kinds of desires and all kinds of aversions, can only be in one place at one time, is vulnerable to illness and accident, and so on and so on. So what is blocking my experience of the consciousness that I am being God, being all there is, is all that I experience of myself to the contrary?

Now, I can in response either say, "Get Thee Behind Me Satan" to all that contrary experience, dissolving it as the nothingness of hypnotism lying about the Truth or I can say, "Enter, for thou art the Son of God knocking at my door through this experience."

In Medieval mysticism it was called via negativa or via positiva. Both are the same. Whether you're telling Satan to beat it or welcoming God in His fullness, either way it amounts to the same thing. Telling Satan to beat it is to see limitation and separateness as nothing. Welcoming God is to see infinity and oneness as all. They're both the same. Seeing infinity and oneness as all automatically sees limitation and separateness as nothing. And seeing limitation and separateness as nothing automatically leaves infinity and oneness as all.

So realize that you are doing both whenever you are doing either. Whether you are nothingizing or welcoming you are doing the same thing. You can't do one without the other. If you welcome an experience as God, everything about the experience that appeared to entail limitation and separateness vanishes. If you nothingize those aspects of an experience that entail limitation and separateness, the experience reveals itself to be God. You never nothingize that which is not God, without in turn welcoming God. And you never welcome God, without having nothingized anything about the experience that appeared to be not God.

Both can be done simultaneously as one act -- what Lillian DeWaters calls "The Act of Truth." And when they are done simultaneously as one "Act of Truth" it can be done all the time. We can at every moment of our lives (which is actually the one timeless and eternal present moment) be both welcoming God and nothingizing any appearance of not God in *every single experience without exception.*

What would qualify as an exception anyway? What

possible experience could possibly warrant being accepted as something less than God? What possible action could possibly be appropriate as our response to the experience except the act of Truth? If we don't welcome the experience as God, then what do we do? Push it away as something other than God? If we don't nothingize anything about the experience that appears to be less than God, then what do we do? Welcome limitation and separateness as God? Seen from this perspective it is utter insanity to relate to any experience at any time in any other way than with the "Act of Truth."

Now, how do we know what it is about an experience that actually is the appearance of something other than God? Having an aversion to something just means that we learned to judge it as evil or bad. It does not mean that it is other than God. So how do we know what's God and what isn't if our own desires and aversions are not the criteria?

We know only to the extent that the principle of infinite oneness is understandable to us. God being all there is, there can be no other and therefore being one, boundless and infinite. It is, in fact, the only intelligible thing intelligence can know. And you are the one and only intelligence that can know it. And when we contemplate the principle in stillness, we do know it, and we know it with absolute certainty. Then it just becomes a matter of using that knowledge as the criterion. Is there something about an experience that appears to be other than infinite and one? Is there something about an experience that appears to be limited and separate? If there appears to be, it is contrary to the only thing that is intelligible -- infinite oneness -- and so we nothingize it and welcome the experience as God -- infinite oneness. We can, and should, be doing it continuously at every moment of the day. Not only is there nothing else worth doing, but anything else we do besides that is creating the illusion of limitation and separation that we long so much to get free of.

Who is this liar? Who is it that deliberately believes that which is not true?

The Brick

What is the key brick to the metanoic wall that will yield a major breakthrough?

Well, let's examine what that brick might be.

God is all there is. That means that you are God and that everything you experience is God without exception. That means that nothing ever happens except God. That means that you never do, think, feel or intend anything other than God.

"But," you say, "I don't experience myself as God." The key brick is to know that that is a lie and that you are lying when you say that. There can't be anything other than God and you can't be anything other than God. There isn't anything for you to experience other than God. So the whole thing is a lie. And hence if you believe it, you are simply lying to yourself.

Who is this liar? Who is it that deliberately believes that which not true? Who is lying, and why is he lying? It is not the self that you actually are that is lying. The self that you actually are is God absolutely aware of himself as all there is. The self of you that believes he is a particular human being named Mr. Ben Gilberti, who has a family and life history. This persona is the central figure in a human drama story, with a physical body that needs protection and all manner of supplies and services. This facade who can own a back account and property and develop financial and/or political power, that can be wealthy or poor, hero or villain, success or failure, healthy or ill, alive or dead. That's the self who would believe he had something to profit from believing the lie, "I don't experience myself as God."

Almost the entirety of the drama this self is playing out in the dream is predicated on the belief "I don't experience myself as God." Take that belief away and that whole self goes, lock, stock and barrel. If that self were to stop telling that lie, it would disappear instantly. It has no existence other than posing as though the lie were true. In so doing it is essential that you do not experience yourself as God or else you wouldn't be able to play the role in the dream at all. If you completely experienced yourself as God you would not be able to not experience yourself as God and act out the drama predicated on that premise. The local self would disappear instantly. The local self is only a lie. The local self is the lie, *I don't experience myself as God, I experience myself as a local self, separate and apart from billions, maybe trillions, of other local selves, each of us with a limited amount of power, intelligence and ability.*

But the answer is still very simple. Simply tell the truth. That's all. In so doing, the self that tells the lie disappears and you return to your true identity -- God. Simply tell the truth, which is: *I experience myself as God.* Contemplate that in meditation. Then contemplate it all the time in a meditation that goes on within you no matter what you may be saying or doing *I experience myself as God.*

Ontological Mysticism   Ben Gilberti

But don't say it as though it were an affirmation. You aren't trying to declare it into being. Say it as though you were simply telling the truth. Feel what it feels like to simply tell the truth. Feel the contrast between that and how it feels to be a liar who tells the lie, *I don't experience myself as God* in order to maintain his own imaginary existence.

Do you really feel like going back to pretending to be that lying self? Of course not! Are you pulled back into it against your will? Of course not,
the local self has no power whatsoever except insofar as someone decides to lie in order to create the local self. Once you simply tell the truth, there is no longer any self that decides to lie instead. The local self comes and goes with the decision to tell the truth or tell a lie. All you have to do is simply tell the truth: *I experience myself as God.*

What you really are is the Father, what you really are is infinite possibility.

The Cosmic Intention: Infinity Resonating as Finite Definition

God wanted to experience himself as something less than himself, and so God goes ahead and experiences himself as something less than himself.

God is infinite possibility, and God is experiencing himself as that infinite possibility when he chooses to experience himself as something finite. The infinite is the Father and the finite is the Son.

But the Father and the Son are One. It is only because of infinite possibility that a particular possibility can have its being. And it is only because all possibilities exist in their particularity that infinite possibility is true. There could be no Father without the Son, nor any Son without the Father. The Father and the Son are ONE. The infinite and the finite are ONE. Without finite particular expression of the infinity of possibility that infinite possibility is, infinite possibility would be a sham. And without infinite possibility (God) being all there is, there could not be the infinite manifestation of particular finite expression.

What you really are is the Father, what you really are is infinite possibility. Because of this you need not feel trapped in your experience of yourself in finite definition; you realize that it is your infinity that is the sole source of the experience of finite definition; you realize that your experience of finite definition arises solely out of your own well of infinite possibility and hence a feeling of limitation is impossible.

As a result, you find yourself experiencing finite definition without feeling limited in any way. When it is infinity that is feeling a finite definition, infinity is experiencing itself as infinity. When it is you as awareness of infinite possibility that feels what it feels like to experience yourself with finite definition, you are experiencing yourself as God.

We're talking about you, remember. You, exactly as you experience yourself right now, are infinite possibility intending to experience this one particular possibility right now. Let go of resisting it, wanting to change it, or judging it in any way. Just experience yourself as God experiencing a self with finite definition and suddenly all that finite definition feels as light as awareness itself, and, to your secondary delight, turns out to be as malleable as awareness itself.

It is only when you've completely let go of wanting to change anything that your being seems to miraculously respond instantly to your slightest intention.

And what will those intentions be in the absence of all those feelings of wanting to change everything all the time? Now that you don't want to change anything any more, what intentions will you have?

The intentions cannot be described, only felt. Feel

what it feels like to be absolutely infinite amidst all this finite definition. Feel what it feels like to be infinitely intelligent amidst the experience of limited intelligence. Feel what it feels like to be omnipresence amidst the experience of being in a particular location. Feel what it feels like to be one with all there is amidst the experience of being a small part of all there is. Feel what it feels like to be the Father amidst the experience of being the Son.

Just as God the Father spoke from the heavens these same words about Jesus at his baptism, you now be still, and know yourself to be God, and say to your self of finite definition: "This is my beloved Son in whom I am well pleased." From this baptism on, the self of you that is finite is forever the beloved Son (finite definition as sacred geometry) of the Father (infinite possibility) and always and forever one with the Father. In this way infinity is reflected in each finite definition, and this is why such finite definition is called sacred geometry.

One's intention then, the intention which, in the absence of all feelings of wanting control, acts instantly and effortlessly on all finite definition, can only be resonant with cosmic intention, or the intention of the Father, or the intention of infinity. The intention of infinity becomes expressed in finite definition. The word is made flesh and dwells amongst us. That is sacred geometry. All then becomes the beloved Son in whom the Father is well pleased.

It will be up to the student to jump. The True Teacher will nudge, but never push.

Terror, Intimacy and the Sacred

A True Teacher will always terrorize his students, because a True Teacher will indeed lead his students to the brink of God and nudge them to jump in. Far from avoiding fear, the True Teacher invites the student to jump into it.

What in God's name could you possibly be afraid of if God is all there is? Nothing! So whatever it is that you fear, you can be sure it is only because you have labeled it in some fearful way, but that it in itself can only be God and hence nothing to be afraid of at all.

It will be up to the student to jump. The True Teacher will nudge, but never push.

What is it that the student jumps into? Very simple really and quite terrifying at first, *surrendering to God.* Then and only then will the local self be *The Beloved Son* in whom the Father is well pleased.

Yes, the finite definition continues, *but only in sacred geometrical alignedt with the Infinite.* When you surrender yourself to God you from then on only intend, and only do, the will of the infinite.

It is a very sacred thing to surrender yourself to God. It is also an extremely intimate thing to do -- far, far more intimate than the most intimate moments you have ever shared with a human lover. This is what we really fear.

This fear, and then the intimacy with God, can only be experienced in meditation.

You know what God is now. And you know now that God is all there is and anything appearing otherwise is nothing at all. You know that now. And you also know that this God we're talking about *already exists right smack dab in the plumb center of all of your dreams of duality as your very own consciousness* --- that it's nothing occult or mysterious to hard to find or hidden --- it's your very own consciousness. Your very own consciousness is this God that is all there is besides which there is nothing else. Your very own consciousness is this God that is always entire, total, complete, perfect, absolute and infinite. You already know that.

But when you contemplate the Truth, *I am experiencing myself as God.* You begin to discover yourself in an act of rapturous, intimate surrender to the ultimate beloved and the ultimate lover, God.

This can no more be described than one can describe the mellifluous delicacy, lightness, rapture and bliss of your first love. All of our puritanical and stiff lipped attitudes come up to be melted, and as all the fear/ aggression drives melt away, a sensuous, exquisitely intimate and overwhelmingly rapturous surrender begins to take place as you open every fiber of your being to being ravished by God.

Remember that first love of yours and how bliss meant nothing other than the idea of melting into the beloved. Remember that? It's that same feeling, only this time the beloved is God, and God turns out to be a far superior lover than that human being you fell in love with once.

The feeling wasn't wrong, just its object. The rapturous bliss associated with erotic love is not wrong. The only thing wrong with the whole thing was to offer that much surrender and dilation of self to a human being. You'll return to love all human beings as God. But that first love was wrong to dilate and open and surrender that much to a human being as a human being. Since God is all there is, it is wrong to love anything but God. The fleeing of love was right, only the object was wrong. And of course it wasn't really "wrong" because in fact the object, as something other than God, was totally an illusory appearance with no existence whatever. It ended in disappointment not because it was wrong in the duality sense of right and wrong, but because you are loving nothing.

Every culture on this planet has created ominous taboos surrounding erotic love, and everyone is terribly confused about it all. So let this clear it up once and for all. The feeling, dilation, the opening up, intimacy, ecstasy, delight, the surrender, the desire to merge, all of this is 100% in alignment with a momentum towards spiritual discovery. All the problems connected with it have to do not with it at all, but with the love object chosen. The only "love object" what will result in its fulfillment is God, only God, and nothing less than God.

So go into your meditations as if you are going into an extremely sacred activity wherein you will be surrendering yourself to become thoroughly intimate and ravished by God. You will not be disappointed as you were in your first love. You will not be frustrated with not being able to fuse and merge with your beloved because this time your beloved is your very own self, the only self you really have, the self of you that is this very minute God and always has been and always will be.

It is so exceptionally sacred and intimate that it seems intrusive to even be writing about it. It needed to be said so that we do not think that the tight attitudes we have developed as a human culture do not apply to loving God. Nonetheless, it is an extremely intimate thing that can only be discovered, never described. Nor does it need to be described. When that first love happened to you long, ago, no one instructed you in how to evoke it, and any description of it you may have encountered previously you thought to be nothing in comparison to what it was really like. Remember that? And remember the exquisite terror that surrounded the prospect of revealing your overwhelming love to your beloved? Remember?

Jump into terror and it turns to exhilaration. That's why the terror associated with revealing overwhelming love already has this exquisite quality to it. These are very sacred things to talk about. We are now on very holy ground indeed. No more need be said. Meditation will reveal all the rest.

We can't just practice the presence through the day. We have to stop and become completely still several times a day.

Kiss and Make Up

How absurd for us to think that we can be disconnected from God. God is not only all there is, but he's all there is as your own actual consciousness. Talk about nearer than hands and feet!

And this is what throws us for a loop. It's not that it's too close to us. or that it isn't reality. It's that it's *closer than we've ever looked before.* It's more intimate than we imagined intimacy could ever be. It disorients us and stirs up new feelings. We become frightened and then run from the fear and deny it.

This is why it is essential to meditate in silence. We can't just *practice the presence* through the day. We have to stop and become completely still several times a day. When we do, each time, we become aware of these new feelings, we experience them without resistance or judgment, and we allow them to dissolve under the authority of the real you who says: Be still, and know that I am God.

If we skip meditations, in a period of time the fears and cover-ups of the fears accumulate until you find it very uncomfortable to sit still. And you may find that a whole day can go by when you've managed to avoid meditating in silence all day.

No matter. The more discomfort, the more you stand to gain. Force yourself, if you have to, to sit still anyway. And then gently begin to welcome those denied feelings that are making you so restless, agitated and anxious. Open up to them. You don't have to analyze them or figure them out or understand them or anything like that; all you have to do is simply feel them. Allow them to present themselves to your awareness without any reaction, without you creating any response. You create no response to them whatsoever. You simply feel them and experience them, totally and completely and unreservedly and with purely neutral attention.

It's your resistance to them that was locking them in place. Once you welcome the experience of them without any push or pull from you; allow yourself to experience them to the fullest extent they loosen up into the pure dream stuff they are. And sometimes dissolve so completely that you can't even recall their being there in the first place.

Maintaining that intimacy with God is essential. And meditation is essential to that maintenance. We have all these countless lover's spats with God, though they are hard to recognize as such because no words or thoughts are involved, only feelings. So several times a day we need to "kiss and make up" with God. In other words we need to get intimate with God again by dilating ourselves to feel our beingness as God, to experience ourselves as God, to surrender to God, to melt or dissolve into God.

And just like lovers will sometimes pout for days before they get around to kissing and making up, we sometimes do the same with God, getting awfully busy so that we can manage only 30 second meditations here and there, but strangely avoiding those longer ones. It's just a lover's spat you're having with God, that's all. Just sit down, kiss and make up.

Open yourself up to feeling everything without any judgment whatsoever. As you allow yourself to feel everything that way, all the formations that were out of alignment with God dissolve and you end up finally with nothing left to feel but God because nothing other than God now remains. Fully experience everything. If it's something that's not God, your full and unreserved experience of it will result in its dissolving. And the more the not-God stuff dissolves, the more you find yourself with just God as the only thing left to experience.

Really loving couples have lots of lover's spats because they keep getting more and more intimate and that keeps touching previously hidden layers of ego. Same thing happens with you and God. Don't think your lover's spats indicate that you are not a good student or anything like that. Quite the contrary, they mean you are getting intimate with God. But on the other hand don't go pouting for days. If it's hard to meditate, that's when you need to meditate the most.

The only reason why you're pouting anyway is because you're holding on to some judgment you have about something that's come up. When you open up, trust and surrender to God, and allow yourself to experience everything without exception without any resistance or judgment whatsoever, when you do that, you discover that all your grudges against God were nothing in the first place. It was all just you holding on to some judgments again. And as you say to those judgments, *be still...* the resistance to feeling and experience that those judgments were creating dissolves, and you find yourself free to experience and feel those things that your judgments were making you push away, and as you feel them in this manner they disappear into God, and you and God are in love once again.

Don't just attempt to feel your own identity by itself, or to feel the world by itself. Instead feel the relationship between you and the world. No identity exists in a vacuum.

How to Begin to
Experience Yourself as God

When you go into meditation and become silent, what reveals itself to you to be felt?

You can feel your body, and sense its position in the room, the house, the world and the universe. You can feel your relationships with the people in your life, your partner, your friends, your business associates, merchants, strangers and all of humanity in general. You can feel what you have contributed to the society of humans that will benefit generations yet unborn. You can feel your narcissism and selfishness, the desire to accumulate personal benefits, and the conflict between your selfishness and your desire to benefit all of humanity. You can feel your uniqueness among humans in that you see the divinity hidden behind humanity's duality stupor, and your sense of parental duty to do world-work meditations and to nothingize the pettiness and compulsions and fear humanity puts on display for you every day.

Eventually it will become clear to you that what you are really doing is feeling the relationship between you and the rest of all there is the relationship between you and all that is not you.

What identity are you creating in your relationship to humanity? Have you presumed that since humanity is illusory your relationship to humanity is insignificant, and have consequently created a relationship of concealed superiority and aloofness, justifying it as "being in the world but not of it.?" Have you presumed that your duty to humanity is a lofty and heroic one that you have fallen far short of fulfilling? Do you work with great persistence at spiritual disciplines yet always feeling somehow inadequate and deviant from the lofty and heroic calling to which you presume you have been summoned?

There are innumerable scenarios possible. The important thing is that it is not necessary to make any judgments about any of them. It ultimately doesn't matter what the nature of the relationship is between you and all that's not you. All that matters is that you get to the place that you can allow yourself to feel that relationship, *and to experience it on its own terms without the overlays of your judgments.*

Feel it as a relationship. Don't just attempt to feel your own identity by itself, or to feel the world by itself. Instead feel the relationship between you and the world. No identity exists in a vacuum. Each identity depends on the kind of world it projects. No projection exists on its own either, but depends on the identity that projects it. Self and non-self are woven together in an inextricably interconnected and interwoven whole. If you nothingize only the self that projects the non-self, or if you nothingize only the non-self projected, the other half of the composite will grow its counterpart back, like an earthworm cut in two. And if you attempt to nothingize anything without allowing yourself to experience it without the resistance caused by your judgments, that resistance by its very nature creates the sense of separation that slices it out of your domain of influence.

Usually you are initially aware only of one side or the other, either an aspect of your own identity or an aspect of the world that identity projects, and have a vested ego-interest in keeping the other side concealed.

The classic example of this is the identity that projects a world populated with what it experiences as contemptible (Jews, homos, niggers, perverts, etc.). In these cases, the identity that projects such a world has judged certain characteristics within itself as contemptible, and in doing so, denies their existence within itself. Projecting them as hateful characteristics in others. Ku Klux Klan members, for example, invariably deny and suppress their own sensuality while finding the evidence of sensuality in black people to be intolerable. But these are extreme examples used for illustration. The point is that any identity, including of course the identity that you maintain, is sustained by the same dynamic, even though in subtler forms.

That which is judged as bad or evil or contemptible or perverse or ugly is denied in oneself and projected as external. This is the "benefit" the ego believes it enjoys in splitting reality into two (self and non-self).

Nothing can be nothingized so long as you continue to believe it is not you because by believing it is something other than you, you have placed it outside of the domain of your jurisdiction.

So you cannot successfully set out with the intention of using your knowledge of God to *clean up your reality*, nothingizing all the awful things about your experience. This will not work because the problem is not all the awful things, the problem is your having labeled them awful, and thereby resisting them and locking them in place as your prison bars. If you hadn't resisted, none of it would have gotten locked in place and you wouldn't have to be working so hard now trying to get free of it all. Judging and resisting is what started the whole problem. So you cannot expect to get out of the problem by nothingizing everything you judge and resist.

It's the most bewildering paradox in the whole world. Only when you completely accept something do you let it free to dissolve. It runs counter to some of our most fundamental duality patterns. In duality, when you completely accept something you want to keep you do not *let it free to dissolve*. And in duality, you work very hard to avoid all the things you judge and resist.

Now we find out that's all backwards. The experience disappears when you totally accept it and experience it completely, while at peace, and without even the slightest hint of judgment or resistance. Why? Because all it ever was in the first place was a particular manifestation of infinite possibility. All it ever was is an experience, nothing more or less. The only purpose of an experience is to be experienced. Once you have fully experienced (without any judgment or resistance) then the purpose of the experience has been fulfilled and it dissolves.

Judgment and resistance hinders our ability to

completely experience. The experience lingers for as long as it takes for the to be finally completely experienced.

It seems so natural to work at all this with the expectation that somehow it is going to enable you to eliminate all that you resist, and we can find ourselves getting very busy nothingizing all that we resist. But if we take that approach, we find that everything we nothingize is always growing back somewhere else. Because the problem never was the thing we resist, rather it always was that we were resisting it in the first place.

Analysis of all this can become quite intricate and complex. But analysis is not what is needed. All that is required is that you go into your meditations and feel your way into all the previously hidden, denied, or resisted aspects of the interwoven composite that constitutes the identity you feel as your self and its relationship to the projections you feel as non-self. What is the nature of your social connection with the world? Again, it doesn't matter what the nature of it is, what matters is that you feel it on its own terms without the overlays of your judgments.

As you let go of judging and resisting experience, you find your life becoming very fluid. No longer resisting anything you neither hold onto anything. It was only your resistance that was holding everything in place and now everything begins to flow. You begin to experience yourself as infinite possibility experiencing infinite possibilities. In other words, you begin to experience yourself as God.

Ontological Mysticism   Ben Gilberti

Conclusion: Open Your Awareness to Infinity

There are no two ways about it. God is all there is, and therefore God is the only presence anywhere, anytime. There isn't anything else too be aware of, if you are aware of something else you are aware of nothing. Every time you remember this in relation to something you are aware of existing is other than God, you are nothingizing. And once you have nothingized everything that appears to be other than God, then, finally, you will be awareness aware of itself as God.

Open your awareness to infinity. Your awareness already is infinite. Open your awareness to what it already is. Be aware of the infinity of your awareness. Be aware of your awareness itself. Notice how incomprehensible it is, how fathomless, how purely miraculous it is that you are aware, and that this awareness, this *I*, is the part of you that is one with God. Don't just contemplate the words contemplate the fact, the reality, that you actually are right now, *not after you are enlightened but right now*, you actually are awareness, and that awareness is right now one with God.

Now good ol' Moses can't point more directly than that. And he can't go any further than that either.

Awareness is right there with you every moment of every day. It never leaves you, it's always perfectly present being what it always is, awareness. *It makes no difference what else you may be aware of, that awareness of yours always remains what it always is, awareness the ability to be aware.* It's nearer than hands and feet and closer than breathing. And it's God. It's what you are. You can't be aware of anything with out it. It couldn't be more obvious, more certain, more absolutely true, that your awareness is. . . . . .one with God.

You start by just being aware that awareness is. But eventually, as you keep doing that, you discover that this awareness of yours is infinite, perfect, absolute, whole, complete, one. It's sitting there, so to speak, being all that right now. All you have to do is be aware of it, rather than aware of all kinds of nightmares contrary to it, the *it* being your own awareness. Stop taking your awareness for granted. Stop feverishly searching everywhere else for what it already is. The Holy Grail is what you already are, and it's the exact opposite of anything mysterious, instead it is the most certain thing about you – is that you exist as awareness. All you have to do is be aware of it. Be Aware of what? Be Aware of awareness. Not aware of all your words and thoughts about awareness, but aware of awareness directly.

Moses tells you exactly what to do, Now that I've taken you this far, turn away from me, turn your awareness away from even your most spiritual words and thoughts, and be aware of what those words and thoughts were about -- be aware of your awareness. Silence is not to sit bored in blackness with scattered thoughts bouncing around. Silence is turning your awareness away from any of that and back on itself. You have total control over what you turn your awareness towards. You are effortlessly capable of sitting still and silently being aware of one thing and one thing only, awareness.

What will happen when you do that? You will discover yourself being aware of God. Will it be obvious to you? Yes. Will you be certain of it? Yes. Will you be able to explain it to anyone else? No. Why? It is impossible to explain infinity. Will it astound you? Yes. Because you will realize that this awareness that you are now spending so much time being aware of, is the only source of all that you are aware of. You realize that this awareness, this most certain and essential part of you, is the one and only source of the entirety of all that you are aware of, the universe. The whole thing, in its totality, is your holographic dream, all of it, all the laws of physics, the grandeur of blades of grass and galaxies, it all exists only in your awareness. It is the exact same awareness of everyone else who is aware. You begin to see that the only other person you ever deal with is you -- the one and only awareness that is.

Moses says, "So go on, now, it's right there, all you have to do is quit doing all these other things in your meditations. Sit there and focus your awareness on the most obvious thing in the world, your own awareness. Stop trying to do anything with it, simply sit there being aware of it. Just sit and be aware of your own awareness. You don't sit there hoping that awareness will consent to grant you awareness of its self. You are awareness. You are being aware of yourself. If anybody is going to grant anything it's going to be YOU because you, as awareness, is all there is. Don't take my word for it. Go and see for yourself."

If you get distracted at first, don't be hard on yourself, it might take some getting used to. But it is simple and easy to do. That's the problem. You're always looking for something to do that's fancier. There's nothing fancy about this. It couldn't possibly be any simpler. You just sit there being aware of your own awareness. If when you do it you at first find yourself continually getting distracted by the pandemonium of things you're used to being aware of other than awareness itself then gently turn your awareness back to itself. Sure, you prepare for the silence each time by reminding yourself that God is all there is. This is for the sake of getting you clear enough so that you can see that this awareness of yours must be this "mystical 'I'" that is one with this God that is all there is.

So now there's nothing left for you to do but to become still and quiet and be aware of your own I. Now there is nothing left for you to do but *to be still and know that I am God*. Moses won't go with you. And you will not be able to come back and get Moses to come along later. You'll never be able to explain it to anyone who hasn't discovered it already. But you will know it more surely than you know the nose on your face.

All that these words and thoughts, or any like it, can do, is tell you were to look. Now you have to look, and keep looking, until you can finally see that it's always been plain as day. It's not hidden. It's not obscure. It's not hard to find. It's not lost. You are not cut off from it. And it doesn't take any time to get to. It is the miracle of your own awareness. Just sit there and behold it. When you get quiet enough you will realize that you are beholding God. The God you are beholding is the awareness that you are, the one awareness that is, the only source of all that is.   You will know it firsthand.

No one can look upon God and live. You will not survive being aware of your own awareness. Everything else you thought you were will disappear as it becomes clearer and clearer that awareness is what you are, the only thing you are, and the only thing there is, you, infinitely.

Ella Wheeler Wilcox put it well when she wrote:

God and I in space alone,
with nobody else in view,
"And where are the people, O Lord,"
I said,
"The earth below and the sky o'erhead,
and the people whom once I knew?"
"That was a dream, " God smiled and said,
"A dream that seemed to be true.
There were no people, living or dead,
There was no earth or sky o'erhead,
There was only myself -- in you.
"Why do I feel no fear," I said,
"Meeting you here this way?
For I have sinned, I know full well,
And is there Heaven and is there Hell,
And is this the Judgement Day?"
"Nay, these were but dreams," the Great God said,
"Dreams that have ceased to be.
There are no such things as fear and sin.
There is no you; you never have been,
There is nothing at all but me."

The End

Colophon

Titles CaslonOpnface BT
Text Georgia
Using Adobe InDesign
Digitally Printed USA

www.onespiritpress.com
onespiritpress@gmail.com

You may contact the author at:
b7gilberti@yahoo.com

Ontological Mysticism   Ben Gilberti